I0220765

MY

FAITHFUL

SAVIOR

Trusting God When He Called
My Son to Serve

MY
FAITHFUL
SAVIOR

A Diary of a Mother's Heart

SUSAN HARING

MIL.SPACE BOOKS
an imprint of W. Brand Publishing

NASHVILLE, TENNESSEE

W. Brand Publishing is committed to publishing works of quality and integrity. In that spirit, we are proud to offer this book to our readers; however, the story, the experiences, and the words are the author's alone and portrayed to the best of their recollection. In some cases, names have been changed to protect the privacy of the people involved.

Copyright ©2025 Susan Haring

All Bible verses cited are in the New King James Version unless otherwise indicated.

All rights reserved. No part of this publication may be reproduced, distributed, or transmitted in any form or by any means, including photocopying, recording, or other electronic or mechanical methods, without the prior written permission of the publisher, except in the case of brief quotations embodied in critical reviews and certain other noncommercial uses permitted by copyright law. For permission requests, write to the publisher, addressed "Attention Permission Request" at the email below.

j.brand@wbrandpub.com

W. Brand Publishing

www.wbrandpub.com

Cover design: JuLee Brand / designchik

Back cover and inside photos: author's personal collection

My Faithful Savior / Susan Haring —1st ed.

Available in Paperback, Kindle, and eBook formats.

PB: 979-8-89503-014-1

eBook: 979-8-89503-015-8

Library of Congress Control Number: 2025901708

CONTENTS

Forethought on Faith..xiii

Introduction 1

Chapter 1: Gift from God....................................... 7

Chapter 2: The Early Years.................................... 13

Chapter 3: Growing and Making Faith His Own............... 19

Chapter 4: God Has Spoken.................................... 25

Chapter 5: Farewell, My Son................................... 33

Chapter 6: Fear Knocks, Faith Answers............................. 45

Chapter 7: The Precious Body of Christ 55

Chapter 8: Silent Night, Holy Night.......................... 61

Chapter 9: Life in Iraq 69

Chapter 10: USA Home Sweet Home.................................... 93

Chapter 11: Not Again! 101

Chapter 12: More Miracles 115

Chapter 13: Mission Accomplished 127

Chapter 14: What If?... 133

Looking Back: God's Specific Directives............................ 143

Encouraging Military Families 147

Epilogue 149

A Few Words from Nate.. 151

Be Mine, Lord Jesus 153

Acknowledgements.. 157

About the Author..159

All Your works shall praise You, O Lord,
And Your saints shall bless You.
They shall speak of the glory of Your
kingdom,
And talk of Your power,
To make known to the sons of men His
mighty acts,
And the glorious majesty of His kingdom.
Your kingdom is an everlasting kingdom,
And Your dominion endures throughout
all generations.

—Psalm 145:10-13

The publication of *My Faithful Savior* is the fulfillment of a childhood dream to someday write for my Jesus.

In 2000, the Lord gave me the title of the book but not until almost 18 years later did the Lord call me to write. It was yet another seven years for this childhood dream to become realized.

This story is a powerful and beautiful witness of God's omnipotent hand moving time and again when my son was serving in the United States Army at the height of the Iraq war.

It begins with my pregnancy and follows Nathan's life through to the end of his military commitment to our country, focusing on his deployment to Iraq.

The diary entries presented reveal a vivid picture of my faith being tried and tested as I clung to God and the promises He gave to me concerning Nathan's life, some even before his birth.

Whether from a military family or not, it is my fervent prayer that every reader will be freshly inspired by the great love and sovereignty of "My Faithful Savior."

First and foremost, to my Lord Jesus Christ, who stood strong with me through all the challenges and who inspired me to tell of His great faithfulness! May I never lose hope in the goodness of God as He conforms me into the image of His Son (Romans 8: 28-29).

To Nathan, without you there would be no story. God taught me so much about His compassionate heart through you.

To my dear friend Lois, who believed God was calling me to write, who encouraged me to share my story, and who also committed to pray for me each day during this project.

FORETHOUGHT ON FAITH

My son Nathan (Nate) believed he was called by God to enlist into the United States Army right out of high school. This was the early 2000s, which meant that my son could be serving at the height of the Iraq War. Now, as a mom, I was not a bit happy that my son may someday be in the line of fire! However, even as upsetting as this career path seemed to me, I knew two things for sure. First, I knew that Nathan had to pursue God's call for his life and not "my call." Second, I knew in the depths of my heart that God was the Sovereign Controller over Nathan's life. God held Nate's very breath in His hand, and He would not allow Nate to depart from this life one second before He had ordained. The second assurance was a great comfort because it reminded me that nothing random could happen to my son. At times, God showed me immediately how I was to pray for a need. Other times, I was to lift my eyes and ask Him to show me what to pray. Occasionally, the Lord dropped a scripture into my mind to guide my prayer and encourage my soul. The important part was that He was leading me.

God also gave me some precious promises to cling to along the way. Although they were tested, I knew the promises were birthed from God Himself.

One night in the late fall of 2004, shortly before Nathan's deployment, I opened my diary and wrote after I wrestled with and questioned God's promises:

I can't merely claim my heart's desire and receive. I must wait on God to show me His will and then claim promises in accordance with His will, what He reveals to me. When God shows me something—when He awakens me in the middle of the night right before my son leaves for Iraq and takes me to journeys of deliverance in the Bible, I believe I have a Word from God, a promise on which I can stand. Why? Because the promise was birthed through God Himself and not me.

That night, I felt scared and lost. I didn't know what to do with my fears, so I got up and went to the only One I knew had the answers. As I talked to Jesus and wept in those early morning hours, my Lord took me on a journey through scriptures, ultimately reassuring me that Nathan was secure with Him.

Even though I believed God's promises to be true, the enemy was still there trying to cast doubt on my son's safety. It became a battle of faith over fear. Praise God, faith won. His Word was sure!

We do face hard questions as we journey with the Lord . . . *Am I willing to accept His higher purposes, even when I am hurting this side of glory? Am I willing to accept God's divine will when I don't get what I think is best? Do I really love God for Who He is, with all my heart, soul, mind, and strength? Do I trust God?*

Richard Wurmbrand, the co-founder of The Voice of the Martyrs ministry, said, "A faith that can be destroyed by suffering is not faith." I believe God will redeem every difficult thing in this life for good as we wait on Him. Some redemption is to be seen on earth, and some is reserved for heaven.

There were times in my life when I clearly knew God's pathway, but it didn't align with my own desire, to say the least. God took me to the cross to remind me that Jesus stayed in the hard place for me, that "having loved His own who were in the world, He loved them to the end" (John 13:1).

Jesus remained on the cross for me, loving me until His final earthly breath.

Was I willing to stay in my hard place for Him? By His grace alone, I was able to say yes. Only as time passed could I see God's redemptive purposes through suffering in my life. I felt so blessed that God, by His mercy, often moved in accordance with my heart's desire for Nathan while he served in the military. Yet, there were many times when I had to believe that God's purposes were higher than my ability to see or understand them. I knew it was still beautiful on God's upper side.

I pray that your own Faith is strengthened as you read about *My Faithful Savior.*

INTRODUCTION

*M*y *Faithful Savior* is the title given to me by the Lord over twenty years ago. It was shelved until I recently heard God speak to my spirit that the time to write my story is now. This story starts with me as a young mom anticipating the birth of my first child, and it journeys through a difficult yet faith-building time when that same precious son enlisted to serve three years in the Army.

My Faithful Savior is about the great love and sovereignty of God, shown to me through His divine hand moving time and again on behalf of my son, Nathan, when he served in the United States Army at the height of the Iraq war in 2004-2005. While Nathan was often in perilous situations while serving in Iraq, my faith continuously reminded me that God is bigger and more powerful than anything he was facing. Nathan's own faith reminded him of the same. I hope this story captures how God still moves miraculously today in souls that are totally committed to Him.

It is my desire that God will put this book in the hands of anyone who needs a fresh perspective of the presence and power of God in this age. If that is you, hopefully you will see that with God at the center of your life, nothing is impossible!

Today I am sixty-four years old, and, like you, I have had many joys and trials in my life, even beyond those I write about in this book. It is the God I have come to know through these very challenging times that I would like to share. He has been my Redeemer and the Blessed Redeemer of every difficult circumstance I have encountered in my life. God has been the Healer, Provider, Comforter, Counselor, Best Friend, and Promise Keeper of my life. He has been the Rock of my life, and because of this I have been inspired to write.

This mother's walk of faith is presented alongside my raw journal entries, displaying a candid picture of God working in my heart. With insight from Nathan himself, it also reveals his faith and how God's power and provision on his behalf was a great witness to others.

I first began journaling shortly after the Lord answered a question that had befuddled me for years: *When in my day can I consistently have a quiet time with my Lord?* I had tried to be in His Presence at various times of the day, but it usually felt as though I had given God my leftovers. By the time I met with Him, I was too tired for it to be quality time.

So, one day in the kitchen, after packing school lunches and while pondering all of this, I asked Him, "Lord, when do You think it is best to have my quiet time with You, because I can't find it?" Immediately, I heard this response in my mind, *"Susan, when do you feel the best in your day?"* I thought about it and realized I felt best around 9:00 a.m., after my oldest two children had gotten on the bus and I'd had my second cup of coffee.

The Lord replied so clearly, *"That is when you spend time with Me."* It was such an obvious answer to give my best to God. I had typically wanted to get as much done with that morning energy as possible, but I knew what to do when I heard God loud and clear and was relieved to have His answer.

Each morning, when the older kids were off and my three-year-old sat in his little rocker watching educational television, for thirty minutes I had my most precious time of the day. I went to my living room and had that second cup of coffee with Jesus. Some days I worshiped and praised, others I poured out my heart to Him and cried, and others I read the Bible or devotionals and journaled my life.

I still diary, and although I continue to refer to these books as my "journals," they are so much more than a place where I record the events of my day. Rather, they are personal diaries of my heart and soul.

My morning meeting with the Lord has been my delight for over thirty years now; it has been the foundation of my spiritual growth. This daily time with Jesus built an intimacy between us that is precious to me. It all began when Nathan was around eight years old, and by the time he was eighteen, it enabled me to release my firstborn into the unknown future with peace.

I began to pray for Nathan while he was in the womb; I later had the privilege of seeing my prayers and the very gifts and dreams God put into my little boy's heart realized in his adult life. I am delighted to share with you an in-depth view of the faith, fears, and joys of this mother's heart at one of the most spiritually challenging times of my life.

I recognize that although there was a happy ending for our family, there may not have been one for many reading this book. For this reason, I've included a final chapter titled, "What If?" This chapter shares my heart for those whose situation didn't end the way they had hoped.

In addition, I offer suggestions that others can use to help support and encourage military families in their sacrifice.

And finally, I've included a "Note from Nate," who shares for himself what his faith in God has meant in his life.

The book ends with "Be Mine, Lord Jesus," which was written to encourage you in your own faith as I share more of mine.

I invite you now to join me on this journey, upon which God revealed to me, time and again, that He is and will always be *My Faithful Savior*. I pray you will be freshly inspired by the way our all-powerful Living God loves us so personally.

For His Glory . . .

For you created my inmost being;

you knit me together in my mother's womb.

*I praise you because I am fearfully and
wonderfully made;*

your works are wonderful,

I know that full well.

My frame was not hidden from you

when I was made in the secret place,

*when I was woven together in the depths of
the earth.*

Your eyes saw my unformed body;

*all the days ordained for me were written
in your book*

before one of them came to be.

—Psalm 139:13-16, NIV

CHAPTER 1

GIFT FROM GOD

Right after my husband and I married, on July 9,
1983, we moved from Ohio to Georgia, far away
from family and friends. My husband, Marc,
had actually been settled in Georgia for three months
while continuing his education to become a chiroprac-
tor. I was excited to join him and to see our first home,
which was a two-bedroom apartment. I also needed a job
to help support us since Marc was in school. God opened
up an opportunity for me to teach at a local Christian
school for the upcoming 1983-1984 academic year.

In April of 1984, my parents visited, and I shared
with my mother how my stomach had been strangely upset. When I went to play tennis with my parents, it was
a concern to my mother because she had more stamina
than I did. However, it didn't take long for my intuitive
mother to come up with the diagnosis: pregnancy!

I actually became so ill in the first several months of
my pregnancy that I had to resign from my teaching position. One morning, after "morning" sickness through
the night, I asked my husband if he could bring me a
Pop-Tart, thinking maybe my stomach could tolerate
it. Frazzled and late for school, he tossed the whole

box of Pop-Tarts across the room to my bed. That left an indelible impression on me—oh, how I missed my nurturing mom! My mom would have toasted the tart, brought it to me on a plate, and stayed to ask what else she could get me. Marc and I laugh about this now, but at that moment I prayed for the child I was carrying to have an exceptionally compassionate heart, like his grandma.

Finally, and with much expectation, on January 16, 1985—more than two weeks past his due date—our beautiful baby boy was born, weighing nine pounds three ounces. I remember the sheer miracle of it all and thinking, *Oh no, I am responsible to do everything for this little life and I don't know how to do anything!* Although I had loved playing with dolls as a child, I had done very little babysitting as a teenager, and the thought of taking this baby home and getting everything right with his feeding, bathing, and more, was daunting to me.

We also had to name this precious baby. We decided to name him Marcus Nathan Haring, III, and we would call him "Nathan." I liked the name Nathan because it meant "gift from God," and I most certainly knew that this child was God's gift to us. I also believed in faith that as Nathan grew, God would reveal to me that my son would have a compassionate heart, just as I had prayed.

In addition, the name Nathan reminded me of the biblical prophet Nathan, who was full of God's wisdom and knowledge and who spoke truth into King David's life. It was my hope that Nathan would also speak truth into other people's lives.

Lastly, I somehow felt this child would have endurance and strength and that he would also be a warrior—a warrior for God's ways and righteousness. God gave me this vision. I would now have to wait and see how God was going to fit all of these attributes together for His destiny in the life of this child.

A man who'll raise the shield of faith, protecting what is pure;

Whose love is tough and gentle; a man whose word is sure.

—Bill Gaither, *"A Few Good Men"*

CHAPTER 2

THE EARLY YEARS

I t was obvious that God had given Nathan a tender heart from an early age. At four years old, Nathan prayed with me to ask Jesus to come into his heart and forgive him of his sins. He was so excited about this decision and still remembers it today.

I remember Nathan at his fifth birthday party when he opened a present of a pair of jeans with a belt. His reaction to the gift was memorable because it seemed atypical for a child. Someone his age might've said "thank you" at his parents' suggestion, and then tossed the gift aside, before moving on to the next. Nathan opened the gift, held up the jeans, made eye contact with the giver, and offered an exuberant, "Thank you! That's just what I wanted." As I look back now, I realize that God had really given Nathan an amazing ability, even at a young age, to be sensitive to others' feelings.

Nathan's best gifts came as siblings. He was thrilled when his little sister, Elizabeth, came along, twenty-one months after him. I remember that when he first gazed at Liz in her bassinet, Nathan let out a shriek of joy and did a happy dance. As she grew, they had a typical brother-sister relationship of friendship and spats.

He was always very protective of Liz, though, rescuing her from a teacher that often wouldn't release Liz in time for the early bus. He would run up to her classroom and tell the teacher that the bus was waiting, and she needed to go! He was actually so relieved to be in another school the following year and to lose that "job."

It was another four and a half years before Nathan's little brother, Christopher, arrived. Nathan was a wonderful, patient big brother, teaching Christopher all he knew about toy guns, the military, airplanes, and hunting. Nathan really was a mentor to Christopher, who had a very teachable spirit. Christopher looked up to Nathan with such respect, and today they remain best friends.

Our family wasn't complete, though, until Alesha arrived. Although she was born three years later, she didn't become part of our family until she was eighteen years old. For many years, God had put on my heart a desire to foster a teenage girl. I just didn't feel done with parenting—like there was more within me to give, but the timing never felt right.

Then, when Christopher was beginning high school and God called me back to teach full time, I assumed, to my disappointment, that God had other plans for me than fostering. Eight years of teaching later, I realized that God had known the whole time the special blessing He had for me at Clear Fork High School. With permission from the administrator, Alesha came to live with us when she turned eighteen, which was early in her senior year of high school. Alesha has been our beautiful, adopted daughter ever since that day! God knew exactly what He was doing when He took me back to my teaching career.

Nathan and his family were visiting us the first night Alesha came to live with us. It was wonderful that we began the journey together as a family. She was welcomed by all, especially Elizabeth, who longed for a sister.

Family parties were always joyful opportunities to gather and celebrate. Our pictures captured so many seasons in our lives. I have a photograph of Nathan that was taken on his third birthday, as he was sitting at the head of a decorated table with a little toy pistol lying above his plate. Like many kids, Nathan loved playing good guys and bad guys with toy guns.

However, I noticed as Nate grew older that his interest in guns did not diminish but rather increased. Nathan's great grandmother told me that her brother had won a gold medallion for being a distinguished marksman. I wondered, *Is God going to give my son that skill? And if He does, how will God use it for good in this world?* This young mom pondered these questions in her heart. I still did not begin to understand what God had in store for my son, whose tender heart came with a fervent desire to defend and protect.

Nathan was about ten years old when he first heard a Gaither song called "A Few Good Men." He would ask me to play it again and again. This was very touching, because I could see the vision the Lord was putting together for my son in this song. Even at Nathan's young age, this song already represented what I saw in him . . . the God-loving, compassionate, brave warrior, who wanted to make a difference in this world for God's Kingdom!

I look back now and see God was preparing me even then for His call on my son's life.

*The Lord will perfect **that** which concerns me . . .*

—Psalm 138:8

CHAPTER 3

GROWING AND MAKING FAITH HIS OWN

E xactly how God was going to fully use this compassionate warrior would remain a mystery for
several years, even though God continued to
show me glimpses of His plan. Nate had many inter-
ests throughout his teen years. He enjoyed football,
airplanes, and anything related to the military. He and
his dad visited Pearl Harbor when we were on vacation in Hawaii. He also enjoyed watching war movies
with his dad, since they both shared a love of history.
Nathan continued to grow in his faith.

One time, when Nathan was thirteen years old, he
visited an out-of-town relative for the weekend and
wanted to see a movie that he felt was questionable. So,
he called home to see if he was allowed to see it. Before
I answered him, God impressed upon me to remind my
son that he knows the Lord and he has the Holy Spirit,
therefore he should go to the Lord with this dilemma
instead of me.

His reaction was, "Oh no, don't do that to me!" He wanted a quick answer, bypassing having to use his own reasoning and conscience before the Lord.

In moments like these, God reminded me that we needed to direct Nathan to look to Him for some of those decisions, so that by the time he left our home he would know God is to whom he is ultimately responsible. We slowly began to transfer the reign of some decisions over to Nathan, always encouraging him to seek God's will, and to our delight, he did.

At fourteen years of age, Nathan decided to be baptized. He had asked Jesus into his heart when he was four years old, but now he wanted to publicly proclaim Jesus as his Savior and Lord of his life. It was such a joy for my husband and me to see Nathan make a public profession of his faith with baptism.

Shortly after being baptized, Nathan got the opportunity to make a short mission trip with his youth group to Puerto Rico. However, this caused a faith issue in me. I vividly recall the difficulty my heart had releasing my son to travel so far without a parent. Shortly before his trip, Nate had an orthodontist appointment. I drove him and was waiting in the car, struggling with the fact that he would be leaving soon, when the Lord spoke to my heart, saying, *"Susan, you are sending your son with Me, your very best Friend."* What tremendous comfort that was, and it gave me peace the whole time he was gone! I no longer had mere "head" knowledge that God would care for him, but I had "heart" knowledge. It brought immediate relief to me to think that I could entrust Nathan and his well-being to my dearest friend—the One, who not only loves him, but who has the power to protect him throughout his trip. It ended up being a very good trip for Nathan. He was able to help with our mission and also witnessed to several teenagers about the Lord through a translator. He came home full of stories and faith.

Nathan was also working through his fears. On his trip home from Puerto Rico there was an inordinate amount of turbulence, which soon after elicited a fear of flying. Later, when our family was going to vacation in Florida for spring break, the thought of flying created a lot of anxiety in Nathan. It was a time in Nathan's life when he recognized that Jesus was the answer and that he really needed to seek the Lord and find peace in the situation through Him. I remember helping him search scriptures and the promises we believed were his to claim. He wrote them in a notebook and took them with him on the plane for comfort. He learned to face his fears knowing that God was completely in control of his life, even when he felt out of control. God gave him the courage he needed, and it was a good trip and a spiritual victory for Nathan. I look back now and see how God was not only growing Nathan step-by-step but also preparing me for the years ahead.

And the child Samuel grew in stature and in favor both with the LORD and men.

—1 Samuel 2:26

CHAPTER 4

GOD HAS SPOKEN . . .

As Nathan approached graduation from high school, I could see that God was preparing my heart to release my precious firstborn son to the destiny He had for him. God's specific call was not clear at that time, but Nathan was interested in exploring military options.

One afternoon, as I was sitting in my family room, I gazed at a potted plant that had been quite beautiful but was recently appearing stressed because I had failed to repot it. I felt the Lord speak to me at that moment, telling me that Nathan needed to be *"transplanted"* and pruned for further growth. God showed me that Nathan had grown to the capacity of his "pot life" at home. We had offered him all we had, and now God wanted to strengthen his faith and move him to the next level.

For Nathan, that seemed to mean military enlistment. Although he had struggled with a physical problem for years beforehand, he really believed that he was to enlist. He had prayed about it and felt divinely guided to commit his physical ailment to the Lord.

I told Nate, "Whatever God calls you to do, He will enable you to do. So, one of two things will happen: If

God has truly called you, as you believe He has, He will completely heal you and enable you. If you continue to have problems, then God has not truly called you there and has another pathway for you to take. It's all about Him."

It wasn't long after this that Nathan decided to join the Army. He enlisted to serve on September 23, 2003, for three years of active duty in the U.S. Army Airborne Infantry. This was difficult for me to hear because of the unrest with wars in the Middle East. However, my husband and I vividly remember what Nathan said coming downstairs one morning while we were watching the news. As he watched the televised commentary on the war in Iraq, Nathan said, "If I had only been a few years older, I could have been there." It broke my heart to realize that the call God had on my son's life, and the desire of my own heart for him, were so different. His father and I knew that as much as we loved him, God loved him even more. He did not belong to us first, but to God, and he needed to fulfill the destiny that God had put in his heart. Nathan needed to accomplish God's purpose for him and his life.

Jesus reassured me that if I sent him to the military, I would once again be sending Nathan with my best friend, just as I had done when Nathan had taken a mission trip to Puerto Rico a few years earlier. This time, I would not only be sending Nathan with Jesus, my best friend, but I'd be sending Nathan with *his* best friend, too. I was so glad that the Lord was faithful to grow Nathan strong in his faith through his teen years.

The Lord continued to remind me not to hinder His will for Nathan's life, and that I must support God's divine plan for him. I thought of Hannah, in the book of Samuel, having to relinquish control of her son to the priest Eli. Even though Samuel had only been three years old, and my son was eighteen, I somehow could commiserate with how she must have felt. I also realized that she could only have done this knowing that Samuel was God's and not her own. I found comfort when I considered God was faithful to protect Samuel from the iniquity around him, and that He blessed Hannah's life for putting Him first . . . for putting His will before her own.

The Lord reminded me that my true love for my son would not be something to get in the way of God's plan. Even though my husband and I love Nathan so much more than anyone here on earth could, God is the author of love and is the One who put the love in my heart for my son. I had to keep reminding myself that Nathan's life journey was with the One who loves him even more than I do. Thank you, Jesus!

I could also see why the Lord had put Nathan in a public school and allowed him to be on the football team. It created the atmosphere where his faith would be challenged before he had to leave home, and where he would need the strength to stand in his faith in the presence of adversity. It also instilled in Nathan physical and spiritual endurance. I believe it created the mentality in him of: "God is with me. I can do it." I recognized that Nathan's strong convictions and faith enabled him to be a positive influencer for God's kingdom, rather than him being negatively influenced by others. This realization brought great comfort to me.

The Lord also showed me, for my own joy, that my focus needed to be on Nathan's future and not what had been left behind. Focusing on the past, or the part of his life that was over, made me sad. But focusing on the future and the bright promise God had in store for him kept me joyful.

Before Nathan even left our home, God gave me scripture verses to claim for him, which were of comfort:

He will guard the feet of His saints.
                                            −1 Samuel 2:9

For the LORD God is a sun and a shield;
The LORD will give grace and glory;
No good thing will He withhold
From those who walk uprightly.
                                            −Psalm 84:11

I also gained insight from the story of David, who in the Bible was called to be a warrior, yet he was still a man after God's own heart. His son Solomon was called to build the new temple, for he had never shed blood in war. These were two God-fearing men who had different callings and purposes fulfilled in their lives by God. Even though the military and the possibility of having to serve our country in war one day was not my plan for Nathan, I fully realized that Nathan needed to be obedient to God's unique call on his life. I also needed to trust that God would give this mom His comfort and His grace the whole way through. The Lord was preparing me for my firstborn to leave home.

The following is an entry of my diary shortly before Nathan left for boot camp:

September 2, 2003
I know I must be brave when Nathan leaves. I know I am not sending him alone but with the Almighty Sovereign God, and my dearest Friend, the Lord Jesus. Still, I will miss the boy—rather, man—such as he is. I love him so much, words can't describe. He is such a picture of gentleness and strength. That must be Christ in him. May Christ shine out of him, Lord, but may darkness be kept away. Lord, surround him with Your angels of protection, clothe him with Your Spiritual armor, and wash him with the blood of Jesus, so that the enemy may not touch him in any way or realm. Guard him and his heart and mind in Christ Jesus. May he find favor in the eyes of his superiors. Hedge him about, preserve him in You, fortify him with Your strength, and draw him even into a closer relationship with You, as You accomplish Your purpose for this time in his life.
    In Jesus' name above all names,
    Amen

He will cover you with His feathers,

And under His wings you shall take refuge.

—*Psalm 91:4*

CHAPTER 5

FAREWELL, MY SON

O n the beautiful day of September 22, 2003, a day that came too soon, Nathan departed for Atlanta. He left for Fort Benning, where he would be for the next several months completing his basic training, infantry training, and U.S. Army Airborne School. I tried to be positive and affirming, but there were still tears. Of course, he tried to comfort me the best he could, but it was hard for me to think that this sensitive son God gave me was soon going to be yelled at by army drill sergeants! My dear daughter Elizabeth reminded me how strong God had made Nathan. I knew she was right.

Nathan said boot camp was a real faith journey for him. He kept remembering what someone told him, that the best way to approach it is to just do all they say and get through it! He said those who tried to quit were not immediately released, but that they had to keep trying to re-enter and finish. He told me that one private who started with Nate and did this very thing, was only on week two of basic training when Nathan finished part one at week nine. Nathan then had a twenty-four-hour leave before continuing on to part two, Advanced

Infantry Training (AIT). Nathan said he really had to keep remembering his goal to be a paratrooper and kept looking at that in his mind's eye, especially as he was filling sandbags for no reason and wondering what in the world was he doing there and how stupid a task it seemed at the moment. Nathan also quickly realized in basic training that the physical condition that had caused him concern was completely resolved. It was a miracle, which strongly confirmed to Nathan that he had indeed been called by God to serve his country.

Nathan said one of the most surprising parts of basic training was the amount of hurry, only for excessive waiting to follow. He knew it was intentional. The trainees would be hurried to the mess hall and then they would be made to stand and wait two hours before proceeding. Or they would hurry to a post to hear the colonel speak and then wait three hours for him to arrive.

The second surprising thing was a bit of culture shock. He had been raised in a small town, had gone to public school, and had played football, but it made me laugh when he said he had never heard so many swear words put together in one sentence than in basic training. Nathan said he felt a deep assurance, though, that God was over this entire process. He had a deep sense of knowing that this was where he was supposed to be, and since he knew that it helped him get through all the hard times.

While Nathan was in basic training, I looked forward to mail delivery more than ever before. Meanwhile, God continued to build faith in me as well. On November

6, 2003, I simply wrote in my diary, "Psalm 91 for Nathan." I knew that it covered themes of protection in the Lord, but I didn't even begin to understand how that psalm would comfort me in the darkness, when I'd later claim every promise. Still, the hope of my child's safety in God held my spirits up, even before I needed His assurances more urgently.

The next night I wrote:

November 7, 2003

You are my Joy, and I can take You, Oh Lord, with me everywhere. There is no place to dread when my Joy goes with me. He puts gladness in our hearts. As we put our trust in God, we can be joyful knowing He is our Defender. God is the Defender and Caretaker of my children. I must release them to Him.

I also quoted an old saint in our church named George, who had had a long life of joy and trials:

George said, "Our life may not go as we plan or think that we want it to go, but we realize down the road that Jesus was holding our hand through it all, and at the end it turns out better than we ever imagined."

When I had held my infant son, I certainly never thought Nathan would be called to enlist in the Army, but George's words were a gentle reminder that the Sovereign God of the universe was now holding the hand of my son and would be faithful to him all the way.

I was so looking forward to seeing Nathan at the basic training graduation ceremony in Fort Benning. However, when my husband and I went to see Nate's graduation ceremony, we could not identify him among those who were also in formation. We searched the faces of each soldier, trying to find our Nathan. We knew he had lost a lot of weight, and with the uniforms and caps they all seemed to blend together. It was a little disconcerting for me that I couldn't even identify my own son! We saw a soldier we thought was Nathan and kept our eyes on him throughout the ceremony—only to later find out it was the wrong guy!

At the end of the ceremony, the parents were dismissed, and I walked to the car a little disillusioned. I also watched the soldiers march in formation down the road back to their barracks. Suddenly, my eye caught the eye of my own son. It was that instant recognition which relieved this mother's soul. I missed him at the ceremony, but I had finally found my son! All was well.

Nathan had a twenty-four-hour leave, and we thoroughly enjoyed being with him during that time, before he had to return for the rest of his Advanced Infantry Training. A few weeks later, we were thrilled to have Nathan home for Christmas. Then we said goodbye once again as he returned to Fort Benning for the next month to complete the Advanced Infantry Training. About a month later, we returned with his brother and sister, and my parents, so that we could all watch his final graduation ceremony. Next, he would begin his adventure in airborne training. It was interesting that my son, who at one time had even been afraid to fly in a plane, would now be trained to jump out of planes. How far the Lord had brought him.

January 26, 2004

Nathan begins airborne school today. We just had the privilege of seeing him graduate from Advanced Infantry Training and had a fun weekend with him at Julie and Craig's (my sister and brother-in-law's) house. A man where I had my photos developed in Georgia told me that Nate will be deployed from Fort Bragg about three weeks after his arrival. I don't know if that is God preparing me or what. I do know Nathan is in the palm of God's hand and nothing can touch him without God allowing it. I want to go back and purchase the soldier with the angel hovering over it that I saw at Hallmark. It will be a good reminder to me of Psalm 91, which I shall pray every day for him if, in fact, he is deployed. My hope and trust are not in where Nathan is but in God Himself and His protective cover over Nathan. My hope is not in a place but in God Himself! The Army may deploy him to Iraq, but God will deploy His holy angels to encamp around him (Psalm 34:7).

February 2, 2004

Today, in my quiet time, the Lord brought to my mind that He is the Lion of the Tribe of Judah and that I can bury my head and all that I am in the mane of the Lion of the Tribe of Judah. He is the Omnipotent and Sovereign One who will move on my children's behalf—He will be their Defender and Protector while I press into Him in faith—He will fight while I rest in faith.

During his infantry training, Nate and several other soldiers were given orders to go to an airborne unit stationed in Fort Wainwright, Alaska, upon successful completion of their infantry and airborne schools. My head knew God had reasons I couldn't see for this distance between us, but my heart felt disappointed. Our family had hoped Nathan would be stationed within driving distance. However, I knew that this plan must be God's best, even though it was contrary to my heart's desire. I continued to try to settle my heart and attitude on this distance between us. Then, a couple of months later, and to my *great* surprise, there was a change. About a week before his graduation from infantry training and before airborne school, the drill sergeants came with new orders from the Army. The drill sergeants told Nathan this rarely happens, but he and several other soldiers had all been reassigned to the 82nd Airborne Division stationed in North Carolina. Joyfully, I received this updated news!

Nathan completed airborne training successfully and I was so grateful that he didn't have to deploy immediately following. The Lord still had more training in Nathan's future before he would serve abroad. Nathan and everyone in his unit were challenged to compete for the Expert Infantry Badge. The prerequisite requirements for competing were exceptional skills in marksmanship and land navigation. The challenge began with a timed twelve-mile ruck march, and one thousand soldiers participated. Whoever succeeded was able to compete for the badge.

Nathan was one of three hundred soldiers who passed all the preliminary requirements. However, passing the timed ruck march was no easy feat! This event had definitely been the most challenging, due to the weather conditions on that North Carolina summer morning. Nathan said he totally saw that God's strength enabled him to complete the challenge. Apparently, his squad leader, Sergeant Midland, saw that too, because when he awarded Nathan the EIB badge he said, "Nathan and Jesus did this."

Nathan told me the timed ruck march was so grueling that he was calling out to the Lord to help him at the end and passed the finish line exactly when time was up. He was then challenged with two weeks of detailed skill testing, being only one of seventy-seven soldiers who received the Expert Infantry Badge. Nathan recognized that it was the Lord who allowed him to obtain this badge and to find favor in the eyes of his leadership.

Soon after receiving his EIB, Nathan was selected to enter the United States Army Sniper School at Fort Benning. Nathan considered this a great honor! Because Nathan was an excellent marksman, he was only one of three E-3s (Private First Class) in his class out of thirty-six soldiers selected for sniper school. Once again, I remembered Nathan's great grandmother, who would talk about the gold medallion her brother was awarded for marksmanship. I often thought maybe that is where Nathan inherited such skill.

As Nathan reflected on his Army experience, he shared with me that sniper school was his favorite specialized training while in the military. He considered it challenging and beneficial knowledge.

During that time, Nathan got the disturbing news that his friend's teammate had been killed in combat in Iraq. He told me that the reality of war felt so close to home at that moment. Nathan couldn't help but wonder what was in store for him if deployed. He shared that he felt peace, though, believing that God had ordained his steps and would protect him.

Sniper training concluded in early September 2004, and our son was given a long leave (September 9-21). Nathan said this was a very refreshing and restorative time for him emotionally, physically, and spiritually. Oh, the joy of this mother's heart when Nathan was on leave to come home! There were many plans for visits, parties and get-togethers with extended family, but what stood out the most to me were two aspects of his time of leave.

The first was the great anticipation and joy of his arrival. Each time I picked him up at the airport or watched his red car come up the driveway, I was just filled with anticipation and happiness to see and hug him again. It was wonderful for our family to have him home once again. Our family so enjoyed listening to Nathan, full of stories and personality in sharing them.

Also memorable was the relief it brought to my soul to just have Nate home with us again. I had prayed for him, and God had kept him safe and strong. I had trusted in God to keep him in the shadow of His wings and God was Faithful in answering my prayers. Each time

Nathan came home, it was a reminder of that, which I received with a grateful heart.

But when this particular visit ended, I had no idea when I hugged Nate and kissed him goodbye that I would not get to see him again for what seemed like a very long time.

A man of God in the will of God is immortal until his work is done.

—John G. Paton, *An Autobiography*

CHAPTER 6

FEAR KNOCKS, FAITH ANSWERS

I love the Christmas season, and I was especially excited for the Christmas of 2004 with the thought of Nathan being home. At the end of November, we were just waiting for Nathan to be given a release to come home for the holiday. I was greatly relieved that his battalion had not yet been called up to serve in Iraq, but amid an ongoing war it did feel like that possibility was always looming.

I was at Walmart on November 30, 2004, and I had just checked out. I was about to walk out of the store when my phone rang. It was Nate, and I was as excited as always to hear from him. However, this time the excitement soon turned to sorrow. He told me that his battalion was on Division Ready Force (DRF) until Friday and that it was probable that he would not be coming home. Rather, he would likely soon be sent to Iraq. I could not even wrap my mind around what he was saying. I stopped walking and sat down on a display platform. I just could not believe the news. So many thoughts were swirling in my mind, and I felt like not one of them was clear. I had readied my heart as much as I could have for this moment, but I realized I still felt so unprepared to hear what he was telling me. To make things worse, not only might he not be home for Christmas, but it wasn't clear if our family would even get to see him before he deployed.

I was in shock as he told me the details. Apparently, his battalion of the 82nd Airborne Division had been called up because of the instability in Baghdad. The Army needed more troops in Baghdad because the area surrounding Haifa Street was totally out of control. Nathan informed me that their mission was "movement to contact," which would basically entail the troops walking the streets of Baghdad and waiting for the enemy to shoot at them to determine the enemy location. I knew I needed to be calm and supportive, while feeling so shocked and disheartened myself. God had been preparing Nathan for this moment and he was ready. He had trained and trained, and now it was time to actually utilize all the training. I knew that I, too, needed to be brave and walk forward in all the promises that God had given me for my son.

That same night, the Lord had an important appointment with me as well. I awakened at 2:30 a.m. unable to sleep, with adrenaline stirring within me as I thought of my son soon deployed to such a violent war zone. I knew God was able to keep him, and I remembered all the scriptures I believed the Lord gave me to pray for my son, but at that moment, in the middle of the night, with my son possibly leaving soon to be on the front lines of war, I needed reassurance. I began to question whether all those promises and scriptures that God had given me were specifically for my son. It was a night that I will forever remember because of the Lord's mercy toward me. My sense of God's knowledge of my thoughts and heart, and of the great tenderness He displayed to me that night will always be etched in my mind.

That morning, the Lord Jesus took me on a journey through the Bible. The word that He kept revealing to me in scripture was "deliverance." By 5:00 a.m., I knew that the Lord was giving a specific promise to me for my son. The promise was that He, the Almighty God, would deliver my son from evil and protect him from harm's way. It was so reassuring that I wrote every one of those scripture references next to Psalm 91 in my Bible, which itself had also become to me a promised psalm from the Lord.

In this next entry, a word from the Lord came unexpectedly and with clarity, as though He was speaking in my ear. (This word of the Lord came while I was crying.)

November 30, 2004 (9:00a.m.)

"I'm crying with you, Susan, but My purposes must be accomplished as you would want them to be. I will keep him."

December 1, 2004 (2:45 a.m.)

I think Nate is on DRF until Friday, because Friday they are leaving. I can barely write it. It will hurt not seeing him again, but I just have to trust in the sovereignty of God . . .

The first sergeant acted like it would be a miracle to be back by March 31st, but I'm asking the Lord to have him back by Easter.

This adventure called "life" is not easy. God and His Word are the only unchanging constants in my life. My heart is saddened now to think we may not even get to spend the weekend with Nate. Is God giving me another heads-up to prepare me? I can't think of any other reason Nate would be on DRF until Friday, when he should be released today, December 1st.

I guess a part of me is weary of hoping for things that don't happen. I am grateful Nate doesn't have to have the anthrax vaccine—they banned it. I really need to get ahold and keep the thought that God loves Nate more than I do, and He is holding him.

*Father, I pray only **Your** Divine purposes, and none of those of the enemy, will be accomplished in Nathan's life by his deployment. You will push back the enemy completely. Lord God, only Your purposes will be accomplished. Your will must be supreme. When He calls, we'll go. It's just that maybe it would be harder to see him only to say goodbye.*

December 1, 2004 (4:40 a.m.)

*Oh Father, that we could somehow have the faith to see Your love in **everything**.*

I journaled these thoughts, based on Isaiah 43:13 and about Nathan being in God's keeping power:

There is none who can deliver out of His hand. God, may Your guardian angels protect Nathan and move his feet away from imminent danger. May Your holy warring angels do a battle in the heavenlies in the spiritual realm so that all of Satan's purposes would be thwarted and completely cast down, and so only God's purposes for Nathan's life would be accomplished.

*Nathan's life is in God's hands—no one can take his life away . . . it is in God's hands. **God holds Nathan's life.** It's up to **Him!** No one can deliver Nathan out of God's hands.*

Indeed before the day was, I am He;
And there is no one who can deliver out of My hand:
I work, and who will reverse it?

—Isaiah 43:13

Because he has set his love upon Me, therefore I will deliver him;
I will set him on high, because he has known My name.

—Psalm 91:14

God will protect Nathan by preparing the way before him. God will set Nathan apart, away from harm's way. Praise the Lord Almighty.

Nothing is impossible with You, Lord.

I often read Psalm 91, personalizing it by adding Nathan's name as I read it. I was so grateful for this sleepless December night, because it was a precious night full of what I believed to be personal promises that I could share with my son from the Lord.

By the next day, it was official. Nathan would deploy to Iraq on December 5, 2004. It all happened so quickly.

He would have to leave for Budapest and then move on to Kuwait, where he and his fellow soldiers would be issued ammunition for their weapons, before continuing to their destination of Baghdad, Iraq. My heart wanted to see him before he left but I could tell he thought that it would just make his leaving all the harder. It broke my own heart to think his family, not wanting him to be alone the night before his deployment, couldn't hug him goodbye.

God took care of that. His best friend, Sam, was stationed nearby and was able to travel to Fort Bragg to hang out with him, watch movies, tell stories, and laugh the night before he left.

December 5, 2004 (11:20 p.m.)
Nathan just called me to say a final farewell. He's locking up his phone and moving to the field airport on base. I can't fully comprehend what's happening. It just seems surreal to me. I struggle not to feel bad that we didn't go see Nate over the weekend, yet I feel we did what we were meant to do. It just doesn't seem right. I am reminded God's ways are not our ways. And our thoughts aren't His, yet as we honor Him to lead our lives, He will make His ways apparent to us. It's up to us to obey. Nathan isn't supposed to fly away until 7:00 a.m. into Budapest, and then to Kuwait, and then to Baghdad, and then to only God knows.

Jesus is Nate's Companion. Jesus is his traveling Companion. He's Nate's Companion in battle, his Companion while sleeping, and his Companion on the road to Baghdad airport. I've sent Nate with my **Best Friend**. *Jesus will watch over and keep him in* **all** *His ways.*

Nate got to spend last night with Sam, so I can certainly see how God provided for Nathan in His way. Nate and Sam had a great time.

Once Nathan was in Baghdad, it wasn't long before my faith in God's promise of safety was tested, as the next journal entry reveals.

December 11, 2004 (8:30 a.m.)

Nathan called last night and said they would be moving out tonight by helicopter to two places. Then they'll be on to their place of combat, where he says there have been 1,100 casualties thus far. I must have faith and stand on God's truth, like that of Psalm 91, and on the deliverance verses the Lord showed me. Nathan is a gift from God, not to be taken away; I must stand in truth.

I also pray he will not be harmed, just as Daniel wasn't harmed in the lion's den nor were Shadrach, Meshach, and Abednego in the fiery furnace. God perfectly preserves his people. I am helpless, but by prayer and that is the absolute truth. God is his Sovereign Protector and Shield. Praise the Lord!

I'm also encouraged that, during my call with Nathan, he revealed how God has brought him reassurance. He said one recent night before bed he was feeling a bit anxious to be facing his first mission, and he asked God to just please give him a word from Him. Nate said he opened his Bible randomly and flashed his light on the verse and it was Psalm 91:10, and he wanted to share that with me to comfort me too. May Nathan stand on that truth. Psalm 91; God's protection in the midst of danger.

On December 15, 2004, my friend Cindy called early in the morning to tell me that she had woken at 5:00 a.m. and had felt strongly called to pray for Nathan. That same morning, I had woken with Isaiah 43:13 continuously moving through my mind, so I claimed that promise for my son.

Nathan called that night and said his battalion had been in a forty-five-minute sustained firefight that day. His sergeant told him that he saw a round strike the barrier behind where Nathan was standing. Nathan did not realize until later that the flash he saw in the window was actually someone shooting at him. It happened so quickly and was so surreal that he didn't even recognize how close the bullet came until after the battle. I could barely comprehend what he was telling me as I was simultaneously fervently thanking the Lord for giving me the promises that He was keeping.

God continued to comfort and encourage my aching heart that He would move my son's feet away from imminent danger. I was so incredibly grateful!

Therefore, do not worry about tomorrow, for tomorrow will worry about its own things. Sufficient for the day is its own trouble.

—Matthew 6:34

From God to my Heart: "Stay in the Day"

CHAPTER 7

THE PRECIOUS BODY OF CHRIST

I found myself needing to cling desperately to God's promises over the next several months. I knew God had spoken to my mind and heart in the middle of the night, even before Nathan's first battle in the field. God assured me that He would deliver him from the enemy and that Nate would be physically protected, and I prayed that he'd also be spiritually protected.

However, the enemy did often try to come in and rob me of my hope and peace. I often sang the song "Voice of Truth" by Casting Crowns as a proclamation of God's truth in the face of Satan's lies. This was fortifying my spirit. I could feel God strengthen my resolve to keep trusting Him as I sang.

Then, one afternoon, while I was mopping the kitchen floor, a little soldier sitting on a shelf suddenly fell to the floor. This happened without any indication of what could have caused it. The enemy was quick to rush into my thoughts, whispering that a soldier had fallen in battle, maybe my son. I stopped mopping, sat down on a stool in the kitchen, put my head down on the counter, and my soul began to despair. Moments after, I could feel the Spirit of the Lord rising in me. Suddenly, I rebuked Satan loudly, "NO—that is a lie!" I came against the lie in the Name of Jesus and proclaimed God's promises to me for my son's safety all over again. God then restored my peace.

This was a pattern to be repeated many times over the course of Nate's deployment. Fear would rush in and then the Spirit of the Lord would raise His standard against it. I could sense this battle within my soul. Praise be to God, though, that every time that fear would rear its ugly head, God would speak His Word and banish it!

My heart was also encouraged greatly by the body of believers that offered support to Nathan and our family in a myriad of ways. Another time of personal struggle was shortly after Nate started his first missions. It was a Sunday morning, and I hadn't heard from him for quite a while and knew he was in danger. At church, a dear sister in the Lord named Christie came to me and cupped my hands in hers and said, "Susan, Nathan is in the Lord's hands; that is where he is right now." She reminded me that *nothing* could touch him there in God's hands. She told me she was pleading the blood of Jesus over him, and that God would keep my son in the palm of His hands. God knew just when I needed comfort and was always there. His mercy and tenderness toward me were priceless. Once again, I noticed that every time the enemy wanted to speak fear and sadness to my soul, the Lord spoke more resoundingly of peace and comfort.

I also regularly attended Monday night prayer meetings at church, where a man named Ted was a mighty prayer warrior. It touched me that the Lord put it on his heart to always ask about and pray for my son. When he prayed, I knew that there was power over the enemy in the Name of Jesus. He would often pray that Nathan would not only be physically safe, but that God would also protect Nathan's mind.

One of the most precious Christmas gifts I have ever received was in the very year of Nathan's deployment in 2004. I was a little early for church one Sunday morning and was making my way to my seat when Scott, one of Nathan's good friends, approached me with a gift. I was surprised that a teenage boy would even think of me at Christmas, although I knew Scott had a compassionate heart like my son. Still, I had no idea what he would ever be giving me. I opened the gift as he was standing there, and it was a bracelet that had my son's name on it, with the charms of a heart and cross. It was just beautiful, and even now, writing this after many years, the memory of that moment still causes tears to well up in my eyes. As I wore the bracelet, it was just another reminder that God was, indeed, with my son. My son knew Jesus as Savior and Lord—represented by the cross—and I knew the heart represented the love of God and our family for Nathan. Despite the thousands of miles that separated us, it helped me feel close to Nathan every time I looked at my wrist.

One evening, as I got out of my car, I looked up to a beautiful, clear starry night. As I gazed at the moon, the thought occurred to me that Nathan could also see that same moon. In some strange way, my soul stirred with a bit of joy at that very thought, and the distance between us seemed not so distant.

And we know that all things work together for good to those who love God,

to those who are called according to His purpose.

—*Romans 8:28*

CHAPTER 8

SILENT NIGHT, HOLY NIGHT

At home, we began preparations for Christmas even though it just wasn't the same. Of one thing I was sure: I wanted to send out a picture of my son to all family and friends as a reminder to pray for him. I still cannot express in words the comfort it was when others told me that they put Nate's picture on the kitchen table or refrigerator and prayed for him daily.

I was also very emotional. Every time I heard the song, "I'll Be Home for Christmas" on the radio, I would begin to cry as I quickly changed the station. I was thinking that since Nate couldn't be with us, our annual Christmas traditions would have to wait until his return. My family at home all agreed. The following journal entry reflects that sentiment:

December 5, 2004

We got a huge live Christmas tree today. I couldn't bear putting up the same old tree without Nathan here. I guess I wanted something alive and desired that the house doesn't look like it does in our traditional Christmases. I wanted to decorate differently and not to hear sappy Christmas songs. It's too hard. It is the most beautiful tree I've seen in a house, though.

I loved the smell of pine from our massive tree that my husband brought home a couple of weeks before Christmas. What I didn't realize, though, is that there are various sizes of tree stands according to the tree size. Our massive tree fell three times before Christmas day! It was already becoming a different Christmas, for sure. I thought, *Wow, Lord, when I said that I wanted this Christmas to be "different," I meant, "different, but still good!"*

In addition to this, there was an ice storm predicted for the week before Christmas. We live in the country and if we experience a power outage, we not only lose our heat but also our well pump does not function. We prepared as much as possible, but we still felt so caught off guard when the ice storm hit. It left us without power, and driving our vehicle out of the mess was not even an option for days. I sat in the family room cuddled up with my two younger children as my husband started a fire in our fireplace. A wave of heaviness and sadness fell over me as the utter disappointment of this season was realized. It was just so disheartening that Nathan wasn't home for Christmas and to know that instead he was in a war zone. I think that reality on top of our own seemingly sad Christmas circumstances suddenly felt too much for this mother's heart to bear.

As I finally lifted my eyes above for solace and perspective, God brought Mary to my mind. God did not give me answers but a story—the whole Christmas story from Mary's perspective. It began to unfold in my mind . . .

Even from Christ's conception, she was faced with adversity. Would her fiancé believe that she was pure and had not been unfaithful to him during their engagement? Would she be shamed by the community? God revealed His truth and plan to Joseph in a dream, and Mary spent much of her own pregnancy away from the community. Mary visited her aunt Elizabeth who was also miraculously with child.

Then, I thought about Mary's baby being due to arrive at seemingly the worst possible time. The government required that she and her husband return to Bethlehem for a census. How would she endure the trip? What if she went into labor on the way?

Mary had to endure that long trip—not in a car or plane—but on a donkey, and right at the end of her pregnancy. Then, finally arriving at their destination and ready to deliver her baby, no room was available anywhere in the city for her to rest! I think in my flesh I would have said, "Do you see us, Lord? Do you care? If we had just arrived earlier there would have been room for us. Now, I have to deliver this baby in a cave with animals and with no decent place for my baby to sleep." God caused me to contrast Mary's trust and faith when her circumstances looked bad with my lack of trust and faith when mine looked bad. Mary was able to believe that the very One who allowed her to conceive Jesus had a perfect plan despite how things looked. Nothing was falling through the cracks of God's sovereignty.

We can clearly see now according to scripture that what appeared to be bad was ordained by God for good. It was necessary for Jesus to be hidden so wicked King Herod could not find Him. God reminded me that *He was* totally in control of every single seemingly trite detail of my life, too. God showed me that even though I may have felt like life was out of control and my plans were falling apart, that He was still on the throne. The Bible never stated that Mary complained. Oh, that I could have had such faith to believe that God was right there, squarely in the midst of that difficult Christmas season.

Remembering Mary's story in this vivid way gave me courage once again to forge ahead in faith, and it reminded me that God has a higher purpose for everything—especially Nathan not being with us that season. I believe God used the remembrance of Mary's plight before Christ's birth to reinvigorate my own faith in the goodness of God. This was a reality check for me to quit complaining. I fully realized that my situation didn't begin to compare to Mary's, but my feeling of life unraveling was. Would I respond in childlike trust? Could I see that there are no accidents in the life of one committed to God?

Because we have the advantage of hindsight in the Christmas story, we can see that God had a plan in every seemingly unfortunate event surrounding Christ's conception and birth. God was faithful to Mary, Joseph, and Jesus through it all. As I considered this, God gently reminded me, yet again, that I could believe He was working for good in all the details of our family's life that Christmas.

We still had no power and no running water, when my sister Julie called on Christmas Eve morning. She and her family who lived in Georgia were visiting my parents in Ohio over the Christmas holiday. It was about one hundred miles north of us. She assured me that if we could somehow get out of town and make the two-and-a-half-hour trip, that they would have a wonderful Christmas meal for our family. We did have an SUV, so after some deliberation, we piled ourselves and all our gifts in the car with a prayer. We knew that if we could just get about a half an hour north of town, the road conditions were supposed to be better. Although initially it was questionable whether we would make it, suddenly the road conditions went from heavy broken chunks of ice to nothing—absolutely nothing. At that very moment, I felt the spiritual battle that had been waging war to dishearten us for days had been defeated. We arrived safely at my parent's home on Christmas Eve. We were just so grateful and relieved to be there and eagerly hoping to hear from our Nathan sometime soon.

My best Christmas gift came at 6:30 a.m. Christmas morning when the phone rang. Nathan called to wish us all a Merry Christmas. I was relieved to hear that he was well and would also have a relatively quiet day. My husband, Marc, shared with Nathan that he had a special gift waiting for him when he came home. Marc had bought him a Kimber 1911 pistol and had it engraved,

"Baghdad, Christmas 2004." To this day, my son regards it as one of the most meaningful gifts he's received.

We were all relieved to hear Nathan would stay at his base Christmas day. Marc, Elizabeth, Christopher, and I were also relieved to have made it safely to Toledo to celebrate with my side of the family. It was certainly a "different" Christmas season.

Be merciful to me, O God, be merciful to me!

For my soul trusts in You;

And in the shadow of Your wings I will make my refuge,

Until these calamities have passed by.

—Psalm 57:1

CHAPTER 9

LIFE IN IRAQ

Shortly after Nathan deployed, I pulled a journal off the shelf that my dear daughter Elizabeth had given me some time before, but that I had never used. The cover read: "Trust in the Lord with All Your Heart." I decided at that very moment that I would use this specific journal for Nathan's commentary on his life in Iraq. Every time Nathan called us, I reached for the journal and, speedily and fervently, wrote all he was saying so I wouldn't miss a thing! Occasionally, I just intently listened and then wrote down everything I could remember after our conversation. This became my *Nathan Deployment Journal*.

The journal pages, captured from December 2004 through March 2005, contain glimpses of particularly fearful times in Nathan's deployment. They document a mixture of startling details Nate shared on our calls and the scriptures or hope that he was clinging to. I will share with you some of the many entries, which clearly show the danger that Nathan and his Bravo Company faced. I've also included some notes I took during the time to help me stay centered. The entries also highlight the faith that God gave Nathan and his anticipation to come home, which grew over the several grueling months of this deployment.

December 7, 2004

Baghdad International Airport. They went there in C-130s, military transport planes.

Camp Victory for two days. Rustic sand floors; not nice, big tents with cots.

The Lord will go before Nathan (based on Deuteronomy 31:8).

December 8, 2004

We'll go in a few days somewhere outside the Green Zone, a more secured area around Baghdad.

Another unit had control of the area but lost it to the enemy. The 82nd Airborne Division will go in and rescue the area.

Nate can't say where he's going, but it's in a helicopter.

Cloudy, rainy, smells bad.

December 10, 2004

Training today.

Leaving tonight to an area where there's been 1,100 casualties.

It's out of control there. God is in control!

December 12, 2004

Took helicopter to another place.

At base Camp Headhunter west of Baghdad.

May call home in four or five days.

Nate believes God will take care of him.
It's cold where he is.
Weapons are zeroed.

Nathan explained to me that "weapons are zeroed" means they are sighted in to hit where the sights are aimed, and that they are zeroed prior to combat operations. My heart sank.

December 15, 2004
While out in Bradley armored vehicles, he was shot at.
Did raids today, can't share more details.
Pray for leadership.
There were two or three mortar attacks on base.
He is keeping a journal of details.
He sounds well, PTL!

December 16, 2004
Went on a mission and got into a big firefight.
Walked the street into a couple of hot spots. Grenades were thrown at them.
A bullet landed close to Nate; Sgt. Midland said Nate was almost shot.
Forty-five minutes of sustained enemy fire. They did not know where it came from.
Nate's unit joined another unit for a mission before they replace them.
It was the most intense fight they'd had in a while.
Nate feels fine.
Has faith God will protect.
Pray for leadership.

December 17, 2004
They had an afternoon mission.
  Grenades were thrown at them.
  Not nearly as bad as yesterday.

December 18th, 2004
Guard post duty today.
  Another mission is coming up.
  Nate doesn't feel well.

Nate later explained that his company's mission was to take control of and occupy a small palace along the Tigris River and Haifa Street, which came to be known as "Predator Palace." They would live there and do missions from there, to resecure that sector of Iraq over the next couple months.

January 1, 2005 (1:15 a.m.)
Twenty-four hours out became forty-eight, and so on. Still out for five days.
  Did guard duty as the new year came in. Set up sandbags, did patrols and raids, and will leave again tomorrow morning.
  Nate's platoon was called to back up a unit under attack—Nate's unit was the Quick Reaction Force (QRF).
  They were clearing houses. Enemy was shooting outside.
  Mortar landed ten feet from the guard—a dud, didn't go off.
  Bad guys pay $100 to kids to throw grenades at Americans.

It's like the Wild West—when gun fights are about to break out, the Iraqi citizens know it and clear the area. It is a sign to the soldiers something is about to happen.

This was a particularly harrowing call. Nate told me he didn't realize before these experiences how evil men could really be. He continued to pray and trust God. He said his unit was successfully pushing the enemy out of their sector.

He noted that many had noticed that he reads the Bible. Nathan prayed that the other soldiers would see him living out his faith. He said he prayed during guard duty because it was stressful. He prayed that evil would be banished or destroyed, or that the enemy would fear and drop weapons and never fight again.

It just seemed unbelievable that my son was in such a violent area of the world! Every time I heard from him, I was so grateful to hear his voice and for God's safe keeping over his life. I also realized that he was not fearful and that God was giving him the grace to withstand the pressure a war zone creates.

January 16, 2005: Nate's Twentieth Birthday!
Nathan called 8:20 a.m. our time.

I sang "Happy Birthday" to him.

He was selected to go with four Navy SEAL snipers on a mission.

Nathan was excited when we spoke. The Navy SEALs had asked for a qualified sniper from his unit, and his leadership had recommended him. When he asked how to address the SEALs, they'd told him to do so by their first names. He'd been given their respect as a fellow sniper. Once at their sniper hide, they'd asked Nathan his opinion about what he would change about their position. He helped set up their position, taking turns on the sniper rifle in observation of the area for enemy presence. Nate's company was doing ground missions at the time. Nate asked a lot of questions. He said it was great having the SEALs attached to his unit while working in their sector. It was Nate's first mission with the SEALs, and more would follow. He enjoyed working with them. I was so glad to talk to him on his twentieth birthday!

January 19, 2005 (6:00 a.m.)

It's been a very violent, harsh week.

Grenades, gunfire, and I'm thankful to be safe.

We spoke about January 17th. Nathan had walked down the street and heard a grenade pop, which sounded like a .22 rifle. He looked to the right and saw a grenade bouncing down the street. He then quickly yelled for guys to take cover and ran to the corner to protect himself from grenades and gunfire. He started firing back. He was told to go in and secure the building. One guy took shrapnel in his leg. One grenade blew up over the platoon sergeant, and Nate said it was a miracle he was okay.

Nathan said a prayer from Psalm 23: "Though I walk through the valley of the shadow of death, I will fear no evil: for Thou art with me." He believed the Lord would protect him.

Nate said the past couple days would be aired on *CBS Evening News,* "Wild West Baghdad," on January 26, 2005. When I asked him what to pray for besides protection, he said for wisdom and for the upcoming elections in Iraq.

January 25, 2005 (7:50 a.m.)

Nate feels fine; the week felt like a blur.

They guarded gates then conducted raids. He's thankful for the prayers.

Nate received a package.

Change of clothes was once a week—now every two weeks!

He misses family. Said he's thinking of chicken enchiladas (his favorite meal I make).

He's excited to come home.

Nate said some Iraqis speak English well. He told me the Iraqi military is impressed that American soldiers can do anything when they get out of the Army. This was just another reason he felt thankful to the Lord for our country. He believed we have a great country and had faith God would protect him.

Nate's jobs varied from day-to-day during this time; there was a lot of guarding of polling places for the first Iraqi elections. Haifa Street had been cleaned up of enemy insurgents. That was a big job, as over one thousand insurgents were in the area at one point.

I could hear it in his voice that Nathan was in an intense place, as he described the seriousness of his current area of operation. He shared that from all the combat experience he'd had, he could differentiate various explosions and gunfire just by sound.

He said he looked forward to the ordinary things in life again. Even if his deployment lasted longer, he'd surely be repositioned in February—just his company. The enjoyable things to experience there were laughing, watching movies with the guys on downtime, and talking about home. He said that when he got home, he wanted to farm with his dad and grow a beard.

Nathan also shared that it's as if his eyes had been blindfolded. He always knew he lived in a good country, but everything was put in perspective when he went to Iraq. The United States is not like the rest of the world. It offers so many freedoms that are taken for granted, and it is so easy to think the rest of the world is like our country when it is not. Nate said, "It would be good for every American to serve their country for a time just to help give them perspective and understanding of how wonderful America truly is."

It was very obvious to me that my son was maturing indeed. He could feel that in himself, and he no longer cared as much what others thought. He expressed appreciation like never before for our country and our freedom.

February 5, 2005 (12:00 a.m.)
Patrol, missions, and observation posts.

Numerous shootouts. Six guys got wounded in his platoon.

Working with Iraqi soldiers in sniper positions.
It's a miracle no one has been killed.

The insurgency got much worse three days before the election and flared up again on February 4th. The day before he went out on mission, a soldier from Nate's platoon asked Nate to pray for him. They walked for four hours and nothing happened—answered prayer! Sadly, one buddy was hit the next day but thankfully survived.

Nate prayed promises and claimed the blood of Jesus. He told me, "Every day is a gift from God—you can't describe it, to have your life threatened each day."

A bit of encouragement came when a chaplain visited before an early mission. Sergeant Midland heard the gospel laid out very well. Nathan thought he may have prayed a salvation prayer.

Nate announced on our next call, "Got Uncle Steve's and Aunt Cindy's $100 PX base exchange card." He was very grateful for it. He had also gotten Oreo and chocolate chip cookies and a very nice letter from my friend Linda in New Jersey. He asked me to share his thanks.

Nathan received so many awesome packages from family and friends and greatly appreciated each and every one of them! (Many more than mentioned in these specific diary entries.) He expressed how packages and letters were such a morale booster. Receiving the mail took his thoughts home for the moment and brought him comfort. It was a great reminder of how thoughtfully remembered and loved he was. Iraq and home felt like such separate worlds.

February 14, 2005 (11:45 a.m.)
He's done with Haifa Street.

He did five patrols and felt sure they would get hit. Not a thing.

They did three missions today, nothing. They came back in an armored vehicle and may do security there and organize.

Though Nathan was finally out of the violent Haifa Street area, he was still conducting combat operations in other areas of Iraq. I was so ready for it to be over!

February 16, 2005
Nate took a nap and felt refreshed, but he shared that someone had walked up to an Iraqi National Guard soldier to give him a hug and had blown himself up, killing them both.

Nate and his unit had gone out and patrolled the area where the suicide bomb had been detonated, just hours before the Iraqi National Guard soldiers were ambushed by the bomber. I was grateful that my son had been protected but surely felt the heaviness that war and death bring!

February 18, 2005
Nate moved to a new base in the International Zone.

No assignment for now, but they may still conduct other operations.

It's a pretty day in Iraq and it smells better outside.

Nate shared that the International Zone (IZ) was a transition area where new units were coming into Iraq and old units were beginning to be processed out. He was still in a combat zone, and they would conduct operations as they came up, but they had no specific assigned mission area. This was a more relaxed situation and Nate could work out, sleep, use phones, and eat on a more regular schedule, similar to when he was stationed at Fort Bragg.

Feb 22, 2005
Keep praying for protection.

A big, improvised explosive device (IED) went off at their gate. They could feel it all the way in their tent area. Keep praying—it's still a dangerous area. He will try to call later in the day to talk to Dad.

Nate said three large, vehicle-borne improvised explosive devices (VBIED) had gone off in their area of operations during the time he was in Iraq. Thankfully, they did not hit his unit, although they sadly killed many innocent civilians and Iraqi soldiers. These VBIEDs were vehicles that had been packed full of explosives and driven into populated areas or military sectors and were detonated by a suicide bomber.

March 2, 2005
Nate did a four-mile run with a friend.
He did well in medical training.
There's lots to tell, but not on unsecured phones.
Keep praying!

Nate had completed medical training with success. During the training, he had been paired with his friend Hamilton, and the two had proved a good working team.

In many areas, Nate excelled. Sergeant Midland said if he stayed in the Infantry, he would make E-5 sergeant. Still, he felt frustrated and was ready to come home.

In other news, he got patches to put on his uniform. One was the Combat Infantry Badge (CIB), which was the highest honor for the Infantry. He also received another 82nd Airborne Division patch to wear as a combat patch on his uniform.

March 7, 2005 (4:15 p.m.)

Mission briefing last night. Air assault mission early today—they raided buildings.

Six helicopters, Navy SEALs. A successful mission.

Returned in armored vehicles, slept, woke up, lifted, and ate dinner.

Tomorrow is the Combat Infantry Badge (CIB) ceremony.

March 8, 2005 (10:30 a.m.)

A general was there to present the CIB.

The general said Nate's unit will be headed home!

Despite the fact that other officers wanted them to stay in Iraq longer, because Nathan's unit had done such a fine job on their mission, the general gave orders for Nathan's unit to return to the United States. The Army wanted to keep them as a Strategic Reserve for the USA, so the general signed orders for them to go home. This was welcome news to Nate, who was very ready to come home. He said he needed a break from everyone and everything and sounded a bit down when we spoke. I think he recognized that he could be relieved, because his deployment was just about over!

I was so anticipating being able to see and wrap my arms around my son again.

All of his phone calls had been pointing to another step closer to home. It was a wonderful relief to me that the day of his USA arrival was approaching.

March 16, 2005 (2:40 p.m.)
Nathan got into Baghdad Airport by helicopter late last night. Everything went well.

They must leave for Kuwait in two days and will stay until they fly into the States as scheduled.

He's really excited to come home. He's feeling fine—he even ran and lifted today.

This call, full of good news, brought me such relief. I had an overwhelming sense of gratitude to the Lord for assuring me that He would protect Nathan from harm and evil before Nate's first mission, and then to see this promise being realized and fulfilled. I was greatly anticipating Nate's homecoming already and felt it had been miraculous that his mission had already been accomplished.

I remembered that Nathan had told me it may be a six-month mission. I had told him that I would pray that he was home by Easter. He'd believed that it was highly improbable, but I still felt led to pray for it. However, I didn't yet have an assurance from the Lord that things would be as I'd hoped.

Then, when I realized I would indeed be embracing my son again on Easter morning, I felt in absolute awe of the Lord's loving kindness towards me. It was such a beautiful reminder of what a personal God we serve!

March 24, 2005 (7:00 a.m.)

Another Battalion had come in yesterday, and the lines for the phone had been too long for him to call.

Tomorrow will be their last full day.

March 26th at 3 a.m. will be customs, then they'll leave at 4 p.m. on the 26th.

Supposed to be in at 4 a.m. the next day to Pope Air Force Base.

I told him I'll have a "Nathan" poster so he can find us.

March 26, 2005 (11:30 p.m.)

They stopped in Germany to refuel, then flew to Maine. Veterans met them in Maine with a welcome reception.

They were so glad to land in the USA! Their plane should arrive earlier than expected, at 3:40 a.m. at Pope Air Force Base.

We are at a hotel in Fayetteville awaiting his arrival.

Nate later shared that the airport in Bangor, Maine was where units returning from deployment flew into first when re-entering the United States. There was a very warm reception from the citizens of that community. They would volunteer to greet incoming soldiers to thank them for their service when returning from overseas. Nate said it was so encouraging to him that those citizens and veterans took the time to greet them and make them feel so appreciated for their service.

Nathan, ready to leave for boot camp on September 22, 2003.

Nathan and I after basic training graduation on December 6, 2003.

The first hug after Nathan's return from Iraq on March 27, 2005.

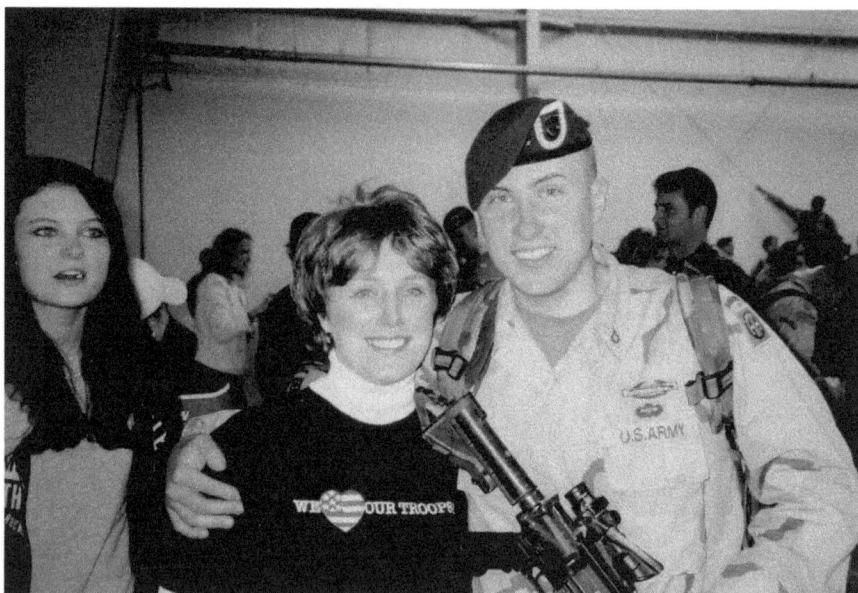

Nathan arrives home safely from Iraq on Easter morning, March 27, 2005.

Nathan and his dad on March 27, 2005.

Nathan and siblings, Elizabeth and Christopher, on March 27, 2005

Home for good! Nathan's final trip up the driveway on September 3, 2006.

The Lord is faithful. Nathan's service in the Army is over,

September 3, 2006.

He who dwells in the secret place of the Most High

Shall abide under the shadow of the Almighty.

—Psalm 91:1

CHAPTER 10

USA HOME SWEET HOME

I praised God on the eve of March 26, 2005, as Nathan and his battalion were en route to return to United States soil! The long-awaited day for this mom was almost here. Since their plane was not expected to arrive until 3:40 a.m. at Pope Air Force Base, my husband, Elizabeth, Christopher, and I were all waiting at a hotel in Fayetteville, North Carolina until around 1:00 a.m. At that time, we made our way to the Air Force Base to greet our beloved son and brother. My heart was so full of anticipation. It seemed incredible to me that the day was finally here.

The following is my journal entry describing the reunion:

March 27, 2005

All I could think of as I saw the plane appear in the air, heading toward the runway, was—faith has become sight! My son is on that plane! He arrived with 270 fellow soldiers. Although Nate's company awarded many purple hearts to the injured, the Lord preserved the life of every one of the Blue Falcons. Not one was lost in battle. Praise the Lord! God had heard the prayers of His people. The Lord is faithful to every promise He gives.

Two generals and one colonel greeted and shook every man's hand to thank them. They remained in formation as everyone entered the hanger, while the Army band played the national anthem. I wanted Nathan to see the red sign we had made for him, WELCOME HOME NATHAN, *held high, Suddenly, I caught his eye and he winked while still in formation. I knew that he had seen us!*

The soldiers were then released to greet those waiting to meet them. I kept holding the sign high so he could follow it to find us amid the crowd. He spotted his family and walked toward me and we gave each other a big hug on Easter morning! What an absolute delight that was for this mother's heart.

"Now to Him who is able to do exceedingly abundantly above all that we ask or think, according to the power that works in us, to Him be glory in the church by Christ Jesus to all generations forever and ever. Amen," (Ephesians 3:20-21).

Praise the Lord!

For months, I'd had to live the scripture, "For we walk by faith, not by sight" (2 Corinthians 5:7), while trusting in God's Word and promises. So, when I finally saw that military plane heading my direction with my son in it, all I could think was, *Faith has become Sight. Praise His Name!* I had an exceedingly thankful heart to the Lord for bringing Nathan safely home!

The most beautiful part of seeing my son again was that, besides noticing that he was physically whole, when I looked into his eyes I could tell it was the same Nathan that had left for Iraq. God had indeed protected his mind as well as his body. Somehow, I knew as I looked into Nathan's eyes right before he hugged me, that the evil he had witnessed in the war zone had miraculously not affected him. It had not penetrated his soul, to the praise and glory of God!

We were able to spend the next couple days with Nathan. Shortly after that, he was allowed to take a leave to come home. We had several welcoming parties with family and friends to celebrate God's faithfulness in bringing our son home safely. It continued to delight my heart that even though Nate had seen so many traumatic events, God truly had guarded his mind as well as his physical body.

When I arrived home, during my morning devotions, I opened my Bible and began to read Psalm 91 recounting God's faithfulness to all of these promises I claimed for my son. I picked up a pen and wrote, "Faith became sight 3/27/2005" in the Bible next to the Psalm. I knew this was the first of two entries I was to make. The other being when I would see his car drive up our long driveway from Ft. Bragg for the very last time. This would be when his commitment to the Army would be fulfilled and completed.

As the days unfolded, Nate began to recount again many of his experiences in Iraq. I was in awe at how God's hand of protection had been over him amid such danger all around him. I also realized that for Nate to do what he was called to do, the Lord had to have dis-armed any fear in my son.

Nate himself expressed amazement when looking back at the courageous heart God gave him to fulfill countless dangerous missions. I also realized the impor-tance it was to my son for him to be a mighty witness for the Lord through it all. He had read his Bible and passed out some tracks to soldiers as the Lord led him, but I was sure that the strongest witness of all was Christ in him. Nathan was able to share his faith with Sergeant Midland before he deployed. Nathan recounted to me that he was able to answer questions and witness to him even more on deployment. Sergeant Midland received the Lord into his life while in Iraq. The following is part of the entry into that little book I kept of my conversations with Nate while in Iraq.

February 11, 2005

Sergeant Midland told Nathan that while he was on guard duty two days ago, in prayer he started asking questions of God. Sergeant Midland prayed and asked God for salvation from sin through his only Savior, Jesus Christ.

Then, he said to Nathan, "Oh, Haring, if you hadn't told me (the salvation message), I wouldn't have known it, if I tell another person, it'll make two."

Nathan also asked us to pray for his sergeant so that the seed planted in his heart would be on fertile soil and grow.

Another time while in Iraq, a friend approached Nathan asking him to lead a prayer for a soldier who was seriously injured. Apparently, the other guys in Nathan's platoon all agreed that they should pray for this wounded soldier and approached Nate to lead the prayer. There was a group of about twenty soldiers wanting to join in prayer. Nathan prayed for the soldier to be healed and that his prayer would be effective. To the amazement of the whole platoon, the man was healed to such a degree overnight that they didn't need to fly him to Germany for further treatment. As my son recounted this, even he sounded surprised by such a miracle. I thought of what a beautiful witness that was to all the soldiers of the living power of God!

Nathan said that he continued to pray the promises of God and claim the blood of Jesus over his own life. I knew Nathan totally recognized that it was the hand of God over his life that had kept him safe.

I marveled at the traits I saw in this son of mine, thinking back to the prayers I prayed for him, even as a little boy; God was now using it all for His glory. God grew Nathan up to be that compassionate, courageous, faith-filled warrior, just like the soldiers portrayed in his favorite childhood song, "A Few Good Men." This all brought such thanksgiving to God and joy to my heart.

I am in God's charge. God is working out my life for me.

—Andrew Murray, *Absolute Surrender*

CHAPTER 11

NOT AGAIN!

It was a wonderful family reunion as we celebrated Nate's safe return home from Iraq. There were many hugs, tears of joy, and prayers of thanksgiving! However, the question that kept looming in my mind was, *Will he be deployed again before the end of his military commitment in September 2006?*

It became my fervent prayer that God would not send Nathan into combat again. I could barely stand the thought of it, yet I knew that if God did call him back to serve overseas, He would impart His grace to my son and also to me. I just wasn't at that place of peace yet and I knew it.

It was time for our annual church family camp. Every July, this has been a highlight of our children's summer. We would pile in the car with all our luggage and head to Huntington, Indiana, where our church family stayed on the college campus for the week. That summer was like all others except Nathan was not joining us. Instead of enjoying the week with us, Nathan was on a challenging, ten-day Army training mission. My thoughts of him were many during the week, thinking often of the rumors that he may have to return to Iraq within the next six months or so. The Lord had been working in my heart to take me to a place of being prepared for whatever God's call would be in Nate's future. The following are journal entries are from that week at church camp:

July 23, 2005

I can see how the Lord has changed my heart over the last month about thoughts of Nathan being redeployed. Initially, to think of the possibility was more than my heart could bear. I came boldly before the Throne and asked God to allow him not to be redeployed. This is still the desire of my heart, but God showed me that danger is here and there for my son, so it matters not where he is but Who holds his life in His hands. The dread and fear were disarmed. I guess the more I'm able to picture God over everything, the smaller everything actually becomes. Now, my prayer is that God's very best would be done in the life of my son. God sees what I can't, so only God knows the best plan. I pray for God's best and that Nathan and all those who love him the most would have prepared hearts.

You are The Sovereign God of Love!

July 25, 2005

Jehovah Jireh, "God will provide." Jehovah Shammah, "God is there." These are two precious names of God to me as a parent. When my children are facing difficult circumstances, like Nate in the field for nine days of training with a 105-degree heat index, and guys are passing out and doing live-fire exercises, I am so grateful knowing God will provide. He will take Nathan over the difficult mountain he faces by increasing his strength, or God will move on his behalf by altering the temperature in the area, changing the minds of leadership, or moving in a way I haven't even considered on behalf of my son. As I pray for strength for him, I think of the passage of Isaiah 40:28-29. God is omnipotent, the ultimate source of all strength. He can supply my children in their times of need. It has been precious to me, praying scripture over my children. God has used this to greatly comfort my own heart; He is there with my son. So, I just thank the Lord that He is right there at that very moment meeting the needs of my children Nathan, Liz, and Christopher.

Have you not known?
Have you not heard?
The everlasting God, the LORD,
The Creator of the ends of the earth,
Neither faints nor is weary.
His understanding is unsearchable.
He gives power to the weak,
And to those who have no might He increases strength.
—Isaiah 40:28-29

July 26, 2005

Every one of our life circumstances as believers is designed to take us closer experientially to our knowledge of God. It has occurred to me that though our trials vary, God's end purpose is the same. What we cling to, what we hold on to tightly, it's as though God takes us on a journey so that our grip is loosened, and we must be willing to relinquish it unto Him.

As I was walking back alone in the rain tonight from our Bible class, I was pondering these things, thinking, "God, truly what then can I cling to? What is it that it is okay to hang onto for dear life and never have to relinquish and be sad? *He said,* "Me." *I was walking on a dimly lit path, when He said,* "You can walk securely with me Susan. I will never leave or forsake you. It is only I who you can, for now through eternity, put all your hope in, and when the road is tough and you do only see that one set of footprints, remember they are mine, as I carry you." *It seems overwhelming, in a way, thinking of Nathan possibly going back to Iraq. He hasn't even been home for four months, and yet I have to prepare to say goodbye again. God keeps asking me,* "Susan, has My arm of protection been shortened?" *God is able. God's comfort has at least always been a step ahead of my need. I praise Him.*

July 27, 2005

"Nathan can do all things through Christ who gives him strength"—I'm inspired by Philippians 4:13, and what Paul wrote in prison about how he could be content in any situation with comfort and much or in distress with little because Jesus' presence is with him.

Nathan: when you feel you're suffering, when you're in the fiery furnace, I pray you remember, somehow—in some way, that Jesus will use it for good.

We are told to be patient in suffering—Christ Himself is our example. The Lord will not give us more hardship than grace to bear it as we look to Him. When we suffer, we must entrust ourselves to Him (God) who judges righteously (1 Peter 2:18-25).

God will see you through, Nathan! The Lord will see you through!

Again, I cling to the psalm: "For the LORD God is a sun and a shield; The LORD will give grace and glory; No good thing will He withhold from those who walk uprightly" (Psalm 84:11).

God always has a purpose for good in our suffering. Look at Christ—He saved all mankind from our sins and now sits at the right hand of the Father, ruling over all principality and power.

I pray for your best, Nathan. Suffering is not meant to destroy us, but rather to allow Jesus to ultimately shine through us more brightly as He conforms us into the image of His Son (Romans 8:29).

God was definitely working in my heart at church camp, and July 28, 2005, was both the most difficult and joyous day of all. I was awakened early in the morning by an unexpected call from Nathan, who was on his ninth day in the field. He'd had little sleep and was struggling through difficult maneuvers, flaring tempers, and just complete exhaustion. He was not quite sure when it would be over. To make matters worse, they were just told that their brigade that they would be leaving for Iraq in thirty days! My mind raced, and I was upset about his situation. It was inconceivable for me to think he would be leaving again, and especially that soon.

After our conversation, I got up to get ready to go to the morning sessions of Bible class. I really could not

keep my mind focused on much of anything that morning except the upsetting news from Nathan. I could not
wait to be released from class at noon, so I could go back
and pick up my portable CD player and take a walk to
clear my mind. I wanted to find a quiet place a little bit
away from the campus to pray and talk to the Lord and
pour my heart out before him. I felt like there were
church people everywhere and although I loved them,
I just really wanted to be outside and alone. I was able
to think of a quiet spot I had seen earlier that had an
open area of grass, with a couple park benches and
some trees apart from the main campus. I had decided that maybe there I would not run into people
I knew and just have a little alone time to process
everything. I didn't walk far before I spotted a park
bench near a fountain.

I sat down and put on my headset and looked around
to make sure nobody would see me so I could finally
release my emotions to the Lord. I saw a woman and
her children across the grassy area, but she stood up
to leave and I was relieved. Finally, nobody was in my
sight. I started listening to the song, "God Will Make a
Way," by Don Moen, believing God would, once again,
make a way for protecting my son in Iraq. As I listened
to it, all of my pent-up emotion came bursting to the
surface. I put my head down and began to sob, when I
heard a sweet voice say to me, "Are you okay? Could I
pray for you?"

I looked up to see the woman from across the park
who had departed with her two children. I thought she
had left, but she had actually circled around the park

and was standing right in front of me. I knew she had been heaven-sent. I was grateful she was from the campus community and not part of our church group. She told me that she and her husband, Nathan, were mentors for the campus students and that they had just recently arrived home from China. She told me the song that I was listening to was a special song to them, as well, as I poured out my heart to her. She took my hand into hers and prayed for Nathan, me, his deployment, and our family. We said goodbye only knowing each other's first names. Although I might not ever see her on earth again, I knew I would see her in heaven someday and just felt so grateful for the body of Christ.

I came back to my dorm room and my daughter, Liz, was waiting to go out to eat lunch with me. When I told her about my day and struggles, she hugged me and said, "Mom, God could do another miracle still and keep Nathan here. Do you remember how he was supposed to be stationed in Alaska after boot camp and then suddenly it was changed to North Carolina?" I agreed with her, yet in my heart I was feeling very doubtful that God had different plans at this stage of the process.

Elizabeth and I went out, she ate, and we walked around a few places in the area before returning to the dorm. She was just getting ready to say goodbye to go up to her dorm room when my cell phone rang. It was Nate. Later on this ninth day, the field training experience was finally over. He was getting in his car to leave for the weekend. He said, "Mom, I'm getting in the car.

I have some good news if you can just wait a minute." Did my heart dare to hope? Tears filled my eyes just thinking of the possibility that the deployment plans had maybe been changed.

Nate then said, "Mom, a company commander spoke with us and said there has been a change. They do still need troops in Iraq for the upcoming election so the Army Corps was told they can choose any division to go except the 82nd Airborne Division. They decided to restructure the 82nd and stop sending them over short-term so that in April 2007, they can deploy a full unit for a longer period of time." Knowing my son's commitment to the Army was done in September 2006, I was elated! I knew God's hand had sovereignly moved. God's mercy to this mother's heart had been so precious. God heard my heart's cry and moved in my son's best interest all at the same time. I praised the Lord for who He is.

There were yet a couple times after this that the Army "changed their mind" again, and Nathan was told he would have to deploy. God had different plans.

August 5, 2005

A new day. Praise the Lord! Nate's jump went well. The brigade commander said there's a 90 percent chance they will go to Iraq in September. I don't believe this. I believe in the Word given to me at a point of despair. God has given me a peace that passes understanding—whatever happens, I am to trust in the goodness of the Lord. He is merciful. I pray the situation of urgency in Iraq will settle, and that the

Marines and Army will have victory and Nathan's feet will remain on American soil. I pray for God's best for Nathan.

My eyes are lifted to God expectantly, knowing He moves the hearts and minds of the leaders. "The king's heart is in the hand of the LORD, Like rivers of water; He turns it wherever He wishes" (Proverbs 21:1). God is in control. My God is able to keep Nate's feet here, but if not, My God is good—blessed be His name. He has given me an unexplainable rest in my spirit.

There is no fear in love; but perfect love casts out fear ...
—1 John 4:18

The Lord spoke to my heart, "Trust in My goodness." I pray for God's goodness in the life of my son.

I would have lost heart, unless I had believed
That I would see the goodness of the LORD
In the land of the living.
—Psalm 27:13

August 10, 2005

And the LORD said to Moses,
"Has the LORD's arm been shortened?". . .
—Numbers 11:23

This verse has been in my mind for some time now while considering Nathan going back to Iraq. I didn't even know where it was in the Bible, and last night when I was feeling a bit discouraged, as I flipped through the pages of my Bible, the Lord allowed my eyes to find it. I wasn't *even thinking or looking for the verse at the time, but God reminded me of this and that nothing is too difficult for him—God has the power to keep Nate on American soil and He has the power to keep him safe while returning to Iraq. I'm not sure how the Lord's hand will move on behalf of Nate, but I do know it will be in one of these two ways.*

Thank you, Lord, for once again encouraging my heart as I turned to You. You truly are my greatest source of comfort.

I love you.

Susan

*Praise God, even when the situation looks bleak, praise God for who **He is**. I won't be discouraged; look at what followed Paul and Silas' mistreatment as they focused on God and not themselves (Acts 16:25-34). We must keep our Focus off us and **on Him**.*

Although at times I was tempted to doubt, I really believed the Lord had spoken peace to my soul that Nate would remain on American soil. I even remember Nathan said, "Mom, we are going," and I disagreed. Only the Lord could give me such a bold stance, yet amid it all, I still allowed an "even if" moment, during which I knew if by some way I was wrong interpreting God's will, that God knows and sees what I do not and that I would walk forward in faith.

August 15, 2005

Just confirmed, that is, the Army has told Nathan's battalion that they could share with their family that they would not go. *The 2nd of the 325th and a battalion of the 504 would go instead of the 3rd of the 325th. As Nathan said, it's a miracle, because the 2nd and 3rd Battalion of the 325th were to go to Iraq in September. Nate said the choice was changed by a "higher up"—yeah, by God's Sovereign hand moving through the Army office!*

I believe this is God ordained. PTL, in accordance with the word given to me at church camp. God gave me a great peace surrounding this decision. God is so faithful—so good—so merciful. He is a God of Miracles! (Proverbs 21:1)

I was incredibly grateful, not only that the decision was changed and final for Nate's battalion to remain on American soil, but also that God spared me from the emotional upheaval. I knew that Nathan would not return to Iraq from God's Word of assurance given to me deep within my soul and that was such a gift from God. It spared this mom from the emotional roller coaster of not knowing what was going to happen during the days of military indecision. Thank you, Jesus!

Now faith is the substance of things hoped for, the evidence of things not seen.

—*Hebrews 11:1*

CHAPTER 12

MORE MIRACLES

I continued to stand in faith that God would keep Nate's feet on American soil. He had a little over a year of active duty service remaining, but even then, he could be called up for an additional five years. Through conversation, Nathan shared with me that he recognized God had divinely protected him physically in Iraq. Since returning to the United States, he had also realized how emotionally preserved he had been throughout his time in Iraq.

That realization became ever-so-evident to him while attending a Christmas party later in the year. There, he found out that several of his buddies were medicated to help them cope with the trauma that they had witnessed on deployment. Nathan felt compassion for his friends, because he realized that he had witnessed and experienced the same things, but by God's grace he had not been emotionally traumatized by them. God had delivered Nathan from evil, just as He'd promised me on that long night I'd been awake with the Lord, just before Nate deployed. At that time, however, I'd thought that the protection would be more in the physical sense, but God had protected his mind as well.

I also remembered how during church prayer meetings, Ted, the prayer warrior, had prayed specifically over Nathan's mind to be protected.

Nathan himself was in awe of God's protective covering and provision for him and realized that nothing was impossible for God. He trusted that God would continue to divinely guide every step of his life as he lived in submission to His will. I realized though that Nathan wasn't just trusting in God for the big things in life, like safety from grenades and bullets flying, but he was also trusting in God's provision for the seemingly smaller things in his life too.

The following entry is an example of just that. Nathan and his friend were heading to church on a Sunday morning:

You are the God who performs miracles; you display your power among the peoples.
—Psalm 77:14, NIV

Nathan called home last Sunday and said, "Hey Mom, do you want to hear about a miracle that happened today?" What mom wouldn't?

He said, "Gwen and I were on our way to church this morning, driving on the highway. All of a sudden, our car quit and I realized we were out of gas. So, I said, 'Gwen we need to pray.' So, we sat and prayed for about a minute, and I tried to start my car. Nothing. I said, 'Gwen, let's pray again.' We prayed for about another minute, then I tried to start the car and it started. We were riding down the road slowly at first then faster and faster, with no gas in the car!

We went for two and a half miles to the next exit and as we got off the exit, the car was dying again, so I said, 'We have to pray now that the car will just keep coasting—let it keep coasting, Lord.' Mom, it coasted into the gas station and stopped right in front of the fuel pump!'"

I was simply overjoyed hearing this story. Not only had God provided for Nate and his friend, but He had given my son a faith to ask for such a miracle. I would have prayed that the Lord would have sent someone along to help me. Not Nate, he had the faith to pray and expect God to help him in a miraculous way and God did. It made me think that God probably loves it when we pray big, because we wouldn't pray big if we didn't know that God could deliver big!

Over the next few days, as I recounted Nathan's story, I realized that God had worked so many miracles during his deployment to Iraq and while in the military that at his young age of twenty-one years, Nathan knew that his God was able! May his faith forever be mighty in You, Oh Lord. Amen!

There was another time when Nathan actually felt very angry at what he considered an unnecessary, painful event that he and his platoon would have to endure, due to what he believed was a terrible idea that the company commander and first sergeant concocted. (This was not the same commander and first sergeant who were in leadership in Iraq: Nathan had much respect for them.) Anyway, it was approximately a fifty-mile nonstop hike from Vermont to West Point on the Appalachian trail. Now Nathan will rise to the occasion if endurance is required for a purpose, but to have his endurance tested simply for endurance's sake was not for him! Needless to say, his opinion didn't matter, and he knew that this trek was inevitable. So, he began to pray for strength and knowledge of how to prepare for such a hike. As I committed this to prayer, the Lord took me to the Israelites' journey into the Promised Land. Scripture tells us that their shoes and clothes never wore out. This became my inspiration in prayer, which is clearly evident, through my journal account of his fifty-mile hike!

August 2006

Do not forget God's faithfulness—Nate shared about his fifty-mile ruck march to Westpoint through the Appalachian mountains. It was a good reminder: The last eight miles were uphill. The sergeant who decided to do this even needed an IV, and he dropped his pack and got a cortisone shot in his knee to finish. God was so faithful in answering prayer that Nate would run and not be weary and walk and not faint.

I had prayed his feet and legs wouldn't wear out, even as the Israelites clothes and shoes didn't wear out when walking in the wilderness for forty years. Nathan said he had even felt well. He kept going and carried some extra weight on his own back for a soldier he felt had been unfairly punished and ordered to carry additional weight.

I had prayed God would hydrate Nathan and give him wisdom and the mind of Christ. Nathan said he could sense God giving him directions along the way, like when to change socks and how much drink to consume. Nathan never needed an IV! So many soldiers were in such bad shape when it was over that Nathan stayed up with the medic to help give IVs for an hour after the march.

God hears and answers prayer.

God strongly supports those whose hearts are loyal to Him (2 Chronicles 16:9).

Thank you, Lord!

There was one more miraculous move of God's hand to literally protect the life of my son while he was serving his final months in the Army. As part of the 82nd Airborne Division, Nathan had to routinely jump out of airplanes. It was unnerving for me each time I knew he had to jump. He told me Paratroopers are not like skydivers. Skydivers have a different parachute that lets them maneuver to land on their feet. Paratroopers' parachutes are meant to get them onto the ground as quickly as possible. Paratroopers are taught to never just land on their feet but to perform a parachute landing fall (PLF), which is a nice way to say, "crash to the ground and roll." Their parachutes cause them to hit the ground between eighteen and twenty-four feet per second, which is equivalent to jumping off a two-story building. But just like Nathan, I had seen God's powerful hand of protection over his life so many times that I committed each jump to the Lord and tried to find rest in that. I say "tried," because I always knew the difference in my spirit between truly releasing a situation to God versus still carrying the weight of it myself. One particular night, I prayed until I really felt a release that God was taking care of my son. Then I went to bed.

However, at around 1:00 a.m., I awoke and knew in my spirit two things. First, I knew that my son was in danger and, second, that God was calling me to get up and intercede for him in prayer.

The following is my journal account of that night:

April 26, 2006

Nathan was scheduled to make his twenty-first jump in North Carolina for a training mission. For some reason, this time I was uncomfortable about this. Nathan told me the weather conditions were predicted to be bad and it would be dark. Around 1 a.m. that jump was scheduled. I also didn't sense much prayer support surrounding Nate's jump this time. I mentioned it to several people, but I felt the Holy Spirit had not really impressed it upon anyone's heart to intercede for him. I also knew that this should not concern me because my ultimate rest had to be in God Himself, and not man.

Before bed, I prayed for him once again and went to sleep. I awoke at 12:50 a.m. to go to the bathroom. I thought of Nathan, got back into bed, and then suddenly just felt an impression to get up and pray. I wondered, is this you leading me, Lord?

I thought it must be, as I remembered times the Lord had given me such a peace that I've slept through his jumps. So, this time I got up. I went downstairs and began to pray for my son, and the more I prayed, the more urgent I actually felt I needed to pray. I had a disturbing impression Nathan was in danger. I continued to pray, especially covering his exit from the aircraft and landing. I didn't know exactly how they were connected, but I kept seeing Nathan having a problem jumping out of the plane. The Holy Spirit didn't reveal to me exactly what it was though. I kept picturing Nathan on the ground hurt and needing help. It was very disturbing to me as his mom.

I began to claim scripture the Lord had given for Nathan. Specifically, I claimed Psalm 91:15-16, referring to those who set their love upon the Lord: "He shall call upon Me, and I will answer him; I will be with him in trouble; I will deliver him and honor him. With long life I will satisfy him and show him My salvation."

My sister-in-law had once told me that my niece Chloe would ask God to send his best guardian angels to protect Nathan when he was serving in Iraq. I thought it was so sweet at the time. I now found myself remembering Chloe's prayer and asking God to do the same and send His guardian angels to bring Nathan gently down, and to especially cover his head and spine. I prayed until I could rest in faith that God was sending His angels to bring Nathan safely down to the ground. I then picked up a hymn book and asked the Lord to give me a song. I opened the book to "I Surrender All." I thought, "Okay God, you want me to surrender Nathan to Your sovereignty and love," *and He gave me the grace to do that. I finally walked up to my room at 2:30 a.m. and went to sleep. I didn't think I would hear from Nathan, possibly for days, because a mission was to follow this early morning jump. However, at 10:00 a.m. that morning the phone rang.*

It was Nathan—this was our conversation:

"Hi, Mom."

"Nathan, how are you?"

"I'm fine. They let us come back to change before we go back out. We've been soaking wet for hours."

"How was the jump, Nate? I was up in prayer for you last night sensing you were in danger."

"Oh Mom, thank you so much for praying. It was the most dangerous, violent jump I ever had. It was dark, we jumped with no visibility into the clouds and rain and when I exited the plane, the wind ripped the helmet off my head! Mom, I just started praying. I knew that I could not hit my head at all when I landed. You can have a concussion and be killed with a helmet, and I didn't even have one. I just kept praying, and as I was approaching the landing, I could feel the wind up on my face and I knew it was pushing me backwards so I made an adjustment to move my body forward to compensate, and I landed feet first in the sand! My head didn't touch the ground.

"Oh, I am so grateful! Nate, at what time did you actually jump? I didn't feel a peace to quit praying until about 2:30 a.m."

"We didn't jump until about 2:25 a.m., Mom. Thank you so much for your prayers."

As I hung up the phone, I was in awe that God had indeed awakened me and called me to prayer, and I was able to participate in how God's sovereignty delivered my son over any desire or power of the enemy. Our God is the **Omnipotent God** of the universe!

I'm glad Nate had not shared this with me before his jump, but he told me later that a paratrooper in the 82nd had died earlier that year after losing his helmet and then hitting his head on landing.

As I pondered this all, I thought *"Who am I? One mom, in the middle of the night, crying out alone to God on her son's behalf, and God heard and answered. How amazing!* It brings tears to my eyes again, as I even write this.

Scripture tells us that God has the hairs of our head numbered and that we are inscribed in the palms of His hands (Luke 12:7, Isaiah 49: 16).

Oh, the absolute wonder of God's love for each one of us. He is intimately acquainted with and cares about every detail of our lives. The Awesome Love of God— Praise His Name!

For all the promises of God in Him are Yes, and in Him Amen, to the glory of God through us.

–2 Corinthians 1:20

CHAPTER 13

MISSION ACCOMPLISHED

Nathan had a particularly trying summer of 2006 while working with his unit at West-point Military Academy. They were training cadets in infantry skills. Nathan was so looking forward to returning home and going to college at The Ohio State University at Mansfield while living at home and working with his father on the farm. As the end of his time in service neared, it seemed to Nathan like the days were becoming longer and longer. Still, Nathan knew his service was almost completed, and he trusted God day by day to help him finish strong. The day was finally approaching for this season of his life to be over. Nathan had just finished that grueling fifty-mile ruck march in August, and shortly after his unit left West Point, New York, and returned to Fort Bragg, North Carolina. He was so ready to be done with his military commitment. I was eagerly awaiting the day that I would be watching Nate's red car drive up our driveway from Fort Bragg for the final time.

September 2, 2006

*Nathan has cleared—got his final papers yesterday. All he has to do is sign out on September 3, 2006. Nathan will be HOME. I've been standing in Faith for the past year that he would not be deployed again and that the Lord would indeed bring him home. God's Hand is never shortened in the lives of His people. God has comforted me and divinely interceded to keep Nate's feet on American soil. He is a compassionate, sovereign God of miracles! He moved in the minds of generals to keep Nathan here. It looked bleak several times over the last year but that's the beauty of our God who calls us to walk by **faith** and not by sight. I believed in my heart the Lord gave me a promise from Him a year ago at church camp when my heart was in utter despair. Nate had just returned from Iraq in March 2005, and they were saying he would deploy again in August 2005. There was then a structural change, and they told Nathan no deployment until spring of '07—Nate would already be cleared! Because I was in such despair when that word came from Nate, I believed God was telling me that my son would not deploy again, period. I have had to stand on that for a year and lift up my eyes unto God and trust. Mercy—God is merciful toward me. I love Him so! My heart can hardly comprehend that the day of his exit from the military is tomorrow. It will mark the end of a very difficult, yet faith-building time. May I never forget God's awesome love for me, my son, and our family, or His miraculous ways!*

Nathan departed from Fort Bragg early in the day on September 3, 2006, and at 8:00 p.m. that evening, we had the pleasure of seeing Nathan drive up our long driveway for the very last time with all of us watching and waiting to welcome him home with hugs and tears!

The following is my journal account of that day:

Monday, September 4, 2006, Labor Day
It was wonderful seeing that red car come up our driveway around 8:00 p.m. last night! It is still sinking into all of us that he is home and doesn't have to go back. This is so good for Christopher, who is starting High School, to have his bro home again! We had a big family breakfast this morning at Nate's request—sausage gravy and biscuits, eggs, and hash browns. It was so nice. Nate's friend Scott just came over to see him. It is a pretty day. We are all planning on having filets for dinner to celebrate. I'm so glad I have today off school. I'm so glad that today I can just relax, worship, praise, and enjoy family.
I Love You, God.
Susan

What a journey of faith for Nathan, our family, and his mom! I opened my Bible to Psalm 91, and next to it I wrote, "T.Y. Jesus 9-3-06." This season of life is finally over! Although extremely difficult at times, the beautiful part was that I could trace the faithful hand of my Savior through all of it!

Praise His Holy Name!

He shall cover you with His feathers,
And under His wings you shall take refuge;
His truth shall be your shield and buckler.
You shall not be afraid of the terror by night,
Nor of the arrow that flies by day,
Nor of the pestilence that walks in darkness,
Nor of the destruction that lays waste at noonday . . .
For He shall give His angels charge over you,
To keep you in all your ways . . .
Because he has set his love upon Me, therefore I will
deliver him;
I will set him on high because he has known My name.
He shall call upon Me, and I will answer him;
I will be with him in trouble;
I will deliver him and honor him.
With long life I will satisfy him,
And show him My salvation.

—Psalm 91: 4-6,11,14-16

These things I have spoken to you, that in Me you may have peace. In the world you will have tribulation; but be of good cheer, I have overcome the world.

—John 16:33

CHAPTER 14

WHAT IF?

I cannot end this book without addressing the question: What if your child did not come back safely from Iraq? What if your child was injured or lost their life? What if he or she physically came back but did not come back emotionally whole? The first thing I want to say is that my heart breaks for you. I do not know why the Lord chose to give me the promises that He did for my son's deliverance. What I have found, though, in my relationship with the Lord, is that there are different promises that God gives.

One is a specific word from Him to my heart that I know in my soul that I can claim as a personal promise from God. This is the sort of promise that I was given for Nathan in the very early morning hours on December 1, 2004, as I read my Bible.

However, I can think of other difficult times in my life that the Lord did not give me a personal promise of deliverance—rather it was a promise of His presence with me despite the outcome of my trial. A trial such as this began years ago following my yearly mammogram.

After several biopsies, I had to have surgery to determine if there was cancer in a very suspicious area.

I think the hardest time of the whole ordeal was the three days I had to wait before the pathology report came back. Although I knew that the Lord would be faithful in my future and that He would use the results for His glory, I had no assurance from the Lord that it would not be cancer. Those three days, when I looked at my future and saw the two divergent pathways my life could take, depending upon what I heard, will forever be etched in my memory. What I knew deep in my soul, though, was that I was to hold on tightly to Jesus, His love for me, and His sovereignty over literally everything! God reminded me deep in my heart that as His child, nothing in my life happened randomly. As I searched God's Word, the Lord pointed me to this promise: "Oh, give thanks to the LORD, for *He* is good! For His mercy *endures* forever" (Psalm 136:1).

Although I was very thankful to hear that pathology results were benign, God had taken me to a place where I knew my soul would be okay because the Sovereign One was working out His best for me. Looking back now, I realize that having that place of peace itself was a gift from God.

Years later, when I had a positive pathology report, His inexplicable peace was also evident, but not until He revealed to me a valuable Truth. I felt like I was at peace with the diagnosis and plan of action until, during that same time, I found out I had Lyme disease. That month, while dealing with Lyme disease and an adverse reaction to its treatment, and while waiting for my cancer surgery, I felt extraordinarily weary. After wandering around in bewilderment, then asking God what to do—because I was unable to make sense of this whole trial—I felt like the Lord showed me how to get through this disheartening time. The word He showed me was "FOCUS." I realized then that fear had entered my soul and caused me to focus on my problems—big, front, and center—while keeping Jesus on the sidelines. God showed me that it needed to be reversed. As I focused on the Lord–BIG, front, and center—through worship and meditating on His precious words to me (which were many and comforting), the unease I felt would be pushed into my peripheral vision instead of in front of me. Although I often sensed how weak my mortal body was, God reminded me that His omnipotent power is in me! He gave me this verse, which I clung to: *"It is* God who arms me with strength and makes my way perfect"* (Psalm 18:32).

God also prepared me beforehand, inspiring me to memorize Psalm 103:1-5. They are beautiful verses. He knew what was coming even though I didn't, and He prepared me through His Word. I felt *hope* and glimpses of *joy* enter my soul once again. God restored my *peace* and lifted my weariness as I focused on Him. After my salvation in Christ, His Peace is the gift I consider most priceless in this life.

My surgery went well. It was three weeks after my surgery before the pathology report came back, so there was a period of waiting and trusting in His plan for me.

Cancer and Lyme disease were mercifully eliminated. If they hadn't been, I would have been a bit surprised, because I felt God had given me some assurance He had healed and delivered me from both. I recognize, though, that I am fallible and God is not. So even if the results had been otherwise, and my perception of what God was telling me was mistaken, it still would have been part of God's agape love for me, since "God is Love" (1 John 5:8) and I am His child.

In the biblical account of the story of Shadrach, Meshach, and Abednego, I believe it was the same for them. They may not have had a complete assurance of how their situation would end, but they fully trusted God for Who He is and pledged their allegiance to Him and Him alone. We know this by their words in the Book of Daniel. They said:

> *If that is the case, our God whom we serve is able to deliver us from the burning fiery furnace, and He will deliver us from your hand, O king. But if not, let it be known to you, O king, that we do not serve your gods, nor will we worship the gold image which you have set up.*
>
> *–Daniel 3:17-18*

These three Godly men knew that God could easily deliver them from what they were to experience, "but if not" they were determined to trust the Lord regardless of the outcome. They knew full well that God *could* deliver! I believe that it is only when we trust God for who *He is*, that we can truly rest, however He moves in our lives, especially when we may feel forsaken.

There was another devastating day, when our family experienced a great loss. What we had hoped for in our hearts at that time was not meant to be. Instead, the

Lord gave me His words, deep within my soul, and they were played over and over again in my mind as a message, I believed, for our whole family, *"Jesus is weeping with you."* Rather than an assurance there would be no loss, the Lord's word was that in our loss, Jesus Himself was beside us, weeping and feeling our pain. The reason for this loss remains a mystery to our family, even after twelve years. Someday, in eternity, when a dark-haired little boy runs up to me and says, "Grandma, I'm Benjamin, your grandson," and throws his arms around me, my broken heart will be restored, and only then will I fully understand God's higher purpose for our family's tragic loss.

The Bible says, "For now we see in a mirror, dimly, but then face to face. Now I know in part, but then I shall know just as I also am known" (1 Corinthians 13:12). Scripture promises that even if our understanding for His high and holy purposes are dim now, that we can trust in heaven all will be evident. We will be able to then see His love behind every painful mystery we have experienced on earth.

In the middle of all the heartbreak, I also witnessed the body of Christ ministering to our family so tenderly that it reminded me of an orchestra, each having their unique part in bringing comfort to our souls. I viewed this as the Lord "loving on us" at our time of despair and I understood more about the tremendous blessing of being part of a church family.

And finally, I remember once in my life that my heart was so numbed by brokenness that I honestly couldn't even feel His presence.

The Bible says, "The LORD will perfect that which concerns me" (Psalm 138:8). When my eyes fell on this verse, it struck a chord in my soul in that I knew it was God's Word for me. Even now, as I look back through my journal, I notice I had written that same verse down repeatedly. However, everything in my life felt so contrary to that verse.

At fifty-four years old, through a series of events, I had never felt so broken. I had the keen awareness that I was broken in every realm—mentally, emotionally, physically, and spiritually– but what was most upsetting to me was that this was the first time I had felt numb spiritually. My cardiologist, who displayed such mercy to this fragile soul, confirmed that my erratic heart was due to tremendous stress. I saw no way out. I felt stuck and walked around in a daze for weeks. I didn't move away from my faith, but I didn't feel especially comforted by it either. I had people pray for me, but the oppression remained.

What I wanted most was to retire from my full-time teaching position to deal with everything, but God had confirmed three times that He hadn't released me. Yet, it was unbearable for me to think of staying. At the same time, God made His will for me clear. He kept impressing upon my mind that He will perfect that which concerns me. I just didn't see it and was weary beyond measure.

After several weeks, Peggy, a lifetime friend of mine, called and after even a short chat with me she told me that she had never seen me in such a depressed state. She asked if she could pray for me against oppression. I said yes, although in my spirit I doubted it would help because others had prayed.

Well, Peggy prayed, and then afterward I told her it was now my turn to pray. You see, as my dear friend was praying, the Lord was showing me that I had slipped into a place of hopelessness and God reminded me of all the words of hopelessness that I had spoken into *my own life*. I needed to repent. I asked the Lord to forgive me and that the spiritual ground that had been gained by the enemy would be taken back. I prayed that from that time forward I would walk in victory. I could literally feel strength in my spirit as I was praying, and afterward the oppression was lifted, and I sensed God was restoring me. God showed me that I could surrender my will to Him, knowing that I was also surrendering my meager strength for His power in my life. The hopeless words I had previously spoken were now in stark contrast to the Power of His strength within me to accomplish His purposes through me. After repenting for the hopeless words, I felt like I could actually pray again and know my prayers were reaching the ears of God. I prayed spiritual warfare prayers that I could not pray before. I sensed spiritual ground gained and my awareness of the presence of God was restored. I say *awareness* because then and only then did I realize He had been with me through my yearlong ordeal, despite that I often did not sense Him in my life.

Even as I write this, I think of Daniel, who was dearly beloved by God and yet there was warfare in the heavenlies, and his prayers had been hindered. Not understanding this, he became very discouraged until an angel came and strengthened him and explained why he was feeling the way he did (Daniel 10). There will be times when we may not understand or feel His presence but just keep walking forward in what you do know and God will help you, because *He is there* with you despite your feelings. We are kept by the power of God through faith according to 1 Peter 1:5. What a comfort that we just need to be in faith and it's up to God to keep us. I believe He is teaching us something through the delays. He keeps us eternally but also keeps us emotionally until our darkened eyes see His light again.

I was finally able to believe the scripture that God would perfect all that which concerns me. What was so beautiful to me is that this promise God had given me was to be realized in the course of about six months. Every burden that I felt was too heavy and inescapable, God lifted and made a way for me! God used this struggle to remind me that my strength is rooted in Christ alone. I would be broken in every realm possible apart from His goodness in my life.

Several months later, a box arrived in the mail. My precious daughter Elizabeth, who faithfully walked with me through it all and fully understood the importance of Psalm 138:8, had the verse beautifully inscribed in wood. It continues to remind me that no matter how tough life may be, God will perfect that which concerns me. As a child of God, He will do the same for you. My daughter and I pass this little wooden etched verse back and forth to each other as we each go through trials and need to be reminded of this truth.

I encourage you right now that if you are in a trial truly testing your limits or if you are suffering a devastating loss, God has not abandoned you. He is there with you in your pain, despite your feelings. Lean hard into Him, for that is the *only place* of true comfort. I have witnessed too often that those who turn away from God become increasingly bitter, leading them even further into a downward spiral of despair and hopelessness. To cleave to Jesus during your darkest moments allows Jesus to apply His healing salve to your soul.

Dear God,

Please tenderly bless all those reading this right now who are experiencing the brokenness and devastation of loss. Draw them unto Yourself, and apply Your healing power to their broken, wounded hearts. Give them the grace to bravely walk forward, knowing You deeply love them and that they do not walk alone. You, oh Jesus, walk with them every step of the way until that joyous day when they shall meet their loved one and You face to face.

In Jesus' name,

Amen

GOD'S SPECIFIC DIRECTIVES

I would like to share with you a few of the directives or impressions the Lord laid upon my own heart during the difficult time of Nathan's deployment. What I find interesting is that these same spiritual lessons that God impressed on my heart can be applied to any trial that you may be going through right now, too! This story of Nathan is to inspire all God's people, regardless of the challenge they may be facing, to lift their own eyes to the Creator who sees them, loves them, and knows every detail of their lives. As you ask God how to apply these same Biblical principles to your own life challenges, I believe He will be faithful to show you.

GOD IS IN CONTROL AND I AM NOT.
This has definitely been lesson Number ONE!

When Nathan entered the "Army world" and then was sent to Iraq, I felt that I could do nothing to directly help my son. I could not be there to help or comfort him, nor could I call the Army and tell them what I thought! It was very frustrating, but was I powerless? No. God called me to pray so that I could see His sovereignty move on behalf of my son. God taught me to turn *every* anxious or disturbing thought into a prayer.

I used to hear Nathan's stories and often got angry with the Army and the way they did things. God began to show me to pray for leadership. I don't have the power, but God does, and if it was in Nate's best interest for change to be made, God would move on his behalf.

I also needed to have heart knowledge, not just head knowledge, that Nathan was not at the mercy of Army rules or men with evil intentions in Iraq, but rather, Nathan was in the hands of the Living God!

I would often recite this verse when the enemy would come and try to elicit fear in my heart: "Indeed before the day was, I *am* He; And there is *no one* who can deliver out of My hand" (Isaiah 43:13).

There is power in the spoken Word of God!

PRAY SCRIPTURE

I asked the Lord to comfort me by His Word. God spoke to my heart through His Word, and I knew I could claim the promises He gave me by faith. It's also a comfort to *thank* the Lord for these promises as a declaration of faith!

For example, "Lord, I praise You that You are a Mighty God, and that Nathan is in Your hand, and according to Isaiah 43:13, there is no one who can deliver out of Your hand."

"WALK BY FAITH AND NOT BY SIGHT."
(2 Corinthians 5:7)

The importance of this scripture had become so very real to me. I needed to stand on who God is and His promises in His Word, and not on how the situation looked. I like the Bible story of Jesus bidding Peter to get out of the boat and walk to Him on the water (Matthew 14:25-33). As soon as Peter took his focus off Jesus and acknowledged the storm, he began to sink. In the same way, I *must* keep my eyes fixed on Jesus, who is the Voice of Truth. The moment I began to entertain fears by letting hopeless thoughts come into my mind, my emotional well-being suffered greatly, and I began to sink. I must recognize the *lie*, come against it in the name of Jesus, and affirm God's truth given to me in His Word, in order to "walk on water." I had to make a choice to look at Jesus and not at the storm. This took a lot of energy on some days and significantly less on others. I could really tell when my sisters and brothers in the Lord were praying for me.

"We are praying for Nathan and your family daily." When someone said that to me, my eyes often welled up with tears. I saw this as the greatest gift anyone could give to us. I regularly prayed God's blessings upon everyone who was uplifting our family in prayer.

One dear sister in the Lord, Joan, who I didn't even know was praying for us, told me with tears in her eyes, "Your family photo is on my kitchen table, and I pray for your family at every meal." I was in awe of this priceless gift to our family. You can truly bless military families by letting them know they are supported by your prayers.

Another sweet thing I heard was, "We want to write to Nathan. What is his address?" It was a tremendous comfort to me to know Nathan had a church family who desired to write to him. A letter or card from home meant so much. It was a short but refreshing escape from his life in Iraq as he read news from home.

Finally, if the Lord lays someone on your heart, let the person know that he/she is close in thought. Cards of encouragement and phone calls all meant so much to me. During a couple of my most difficult days, I felt too sad to call anyone. I felt as though I was grieving the loss of Nathan's presence for a time. I just prayed God would put on someone's heart to call if she were to help me through. On one of those days my sister, who is a teacher, had to run errands in the middle of the day and called me. What an earful she got! But what a comfort to me.

Another day, a good friend asked if I wanted her to come over. I didn't even know what I wanted. She just showed up, and the visit was just what I needed—with a hug, a word of encouragement, and a prayer. At other times, the phone would ring just because God put our family on someone's heart, and I was so blessed! What a precious gift the body of Christ has been to me.

It is my prayer that by sharing these thoughts with you, the Lord will bless and encourage you in some way and challenge you to reach out in ministry to military families that the Lord puts in your own pathway. May God give us all the grace to stand on Him and His timeless Word, Our Forever Sure Foundation. Praise be to His holy name!

EPILOGUE

Nathan returned home from the Army very ready to pursue his civilian life. He enrolled in college and became active in campus ministry, where he ultimately met his bride-to-be, Jorai.

Although we didn't like to think about it, we all knew that Nathan was still considered on inactive military duty for five additional years. He could be emergency recalled to active duty. We tried to not dwell on that possibility, but that is exactly what happened after his second year at home.

During this time, Nate's dad fractured his foot in a farming accident and was unable to walk. Although it was unfortunate that his dad injured his foot, we could see how God powerfully used this circumstance. The Army considered the situation and released Nathan from additional military service so he could stay home and help his family. Once again, God's mighty hand was evident!

Nathan continued to pursue a degree from OSU, all the while deepening his relationship with Jorai. They courted for a year and married on October 10, 2009. We were thrilled to have Jorai become part of our family. I recognized that she was a perfect fit for my son and believed that he would be a true blessing to her as well. They presently live in a small community in Ohio.

Nathan has pursued a career in law enforcement and also works in a family business.

Nathan and Jorai have been blessed with four children: Leanna, Jason, Lucas, and Grant. They have a wonderful church family, and it is a delight for this grandma to see her grandchildren grow up to love Jesus!

A FEW WORDS FROM NATE

As I read this book that my mother wrote of her journey of faith during my time in the military, I was reminded again how blessed I was and am to have a mother who cares so much for me.

I knew Mom was always praying for me in Iraq and during my military service, and she continues to today. I remember as a child waking up in the morning and coming down the stairs to see my mom reading her Bible and having a quiet time. It left an impression upon me at a young age about the importance of spending time with the Lord and having a relationship with Him.

After the military, I was blessed with a wonderful wife and four precious children. I currently reside in Ohio with them and continue to count the many blessings of living in this great country that so many have sacrificed for. Many have given everything in service for our country. We have privileges here that many countries around the world do not. While not perfect, America is most able to help other countries when we are at our strongest. I pray our Nation will turn to the Lord.

I pray this book is a blessing to you as you read about God's faithfulness to my mother and His blessing of protection for me. This book is about Him, our glorious Savior, who has secured for us an inheritance that will never fade in heaven, where we'll be with Him for all eternity. I pray you know Him as my mother, and I know Him and that you would trust Him as your Savior. To Him be the glory, forever and ever. Amen.

BE MINE, LORD JESUS

Aftstyle... **A**fter I finished writing this book, I woke up early one morning with these repetitive words in my mind . . . *I am Yours and You are mine.* I turned to the Lord about this precious truth that was in my mind and on my lips. God revealed to me that I should not end this book without sharing with those reading, who may not know the Lord personally, how they may invite Jesus into their own lives.

I share with you some scriptures that have meant so much in pointing me to Truth:

For all have sinned and fall short of the glory of God.
—Romans 3:23

For the wages of sin is death, but the gift of God is eternal life in Christ Jesus our Lord.
—Romans 6: 23

For He made Him who knew no sin to be sin for us, that we might become the righteousness of God in Him.
—2 Corinthians 5:21

For God so loved the world that He gave His only begotten Son, that whoever believes in Him should not perish but have everlasting life.

—John 3:16

And this is the testimony: that God has given us eternal life, and this life is in His Son. He who has the Son has life; he who does not have the Son of God does not have life. These things I have written to you who believe in the name of the Son of God, that you may know that you have eternal life, and that you may continue to believe in the name of the Son of God.

—1 John 5:11-13

But as many as received Him, to them He gave the right to become the children of God, to those who believe in His Name; who were born, not of blood, nor of the will of the flesh, nor of the will of man, but of God.

—John 1:12-13

Behold, I stand at the door and knock. If anyone hears My voice and opens the door, I will come in to him and dine with him, and he with Me.

—Revelation 3:20

. . . and He died for all, that those who live should live no longer for themselves, but for Him who died for them and rose again.

—2 Corinthians 5:15

For we have become partakers of Christ if we hold
the beginning of our confidence steadfast to the end.
                                    —Hebrews 3:14

When sin entered the world through Adam, it began a sin separation between humanity and God. The Old Testament reveals man's inability to save himself; it also points to the coming Messiah, who once and forever bridges that sin gap between God and man. Jesus is the sinless Son of God. Jesus is called "Emmanuel," which means "God with us," sent here to willingly lay down His life to redeem mankind. It is for us to acknowledge our sin and recognize out of God's great love that Jesus died for us, so that we can be reconciled to God through Him. To accept or to reject Christ is a choice we each must personally make. There is no middle ground.

He who believes that Jesus is the only Son of God who came to earth for the purpose of dying on the cross for their sins, repents, and chooses to receive and follow Him, is the one who is spiritually born again. Jesus will be their ever-abiding companion on earth, and then they will be in His forever Presence upon their last earthly breath.

If this is your heart's desire, you may ask Him to be yours, too, through this prayer:

Thank You, God, for Your Son, Jesus Christ. Thank You, Jesus, for Your willingness to come to earth for the purpose of dying for my sins. I confess that I need You as my Savior. I repent from my sins, and now I would like to receive the gift of Your presence, the Holy Spirit, into my life. From this moment forward, I want to live my life for You, Lord Jesus. When this life is over, my life will not cease, but I will continue living in Your ever presence according to Your Word: "I am the resurrection and the life, He who believes in Me, though he may die, he shall live. And whoever lives and believes in Me shall never die" (John 11:25-26).

Thank You, Jesus, that from this moment forward, I am forever Yours and You are mine; may I now share this gift of salvation with others for Your Kingdom purposes!
Amen.

ACKNOWLEDGEMENTS

To Virginia, thank you for your exceptional editing skills and especially for your encouragement every step of the way. You were such an integral part of God's plan for this project. You always pointed me in the right direction. I can't thank you enough!

S usan Haring is a woman of deep faith and un-wavering dedication to serving others. While raising her children, Susan also loved volun-teering to help those in need. She supported women at a local pregnancy center, advocated for vulner-able youth as a Court Appointed Special Advocate (C.A.S.A.), and mentored high school students. By God's grace, she has devoted her life to encouraging and uplifting those in need.

Susan also served on the Women's Ministry Board at her church, a further reflection of her passion for fos-tering community and faith.

Writing *My Faithful Savior* is another extension of that calling—a powerful testimony of God's miraculous hand in her son's life and His boundless love for all His children. Susan prays that this true story will inspire and strengthen the faith of those who read it.

When she's not writing or serving others, Susan appreciates the simple joys of life—sipping coffee with friends, offering a listening ear to those who are hurting, snuggling with her grandchildren, and baking their often requested chocolate cake.

One childhood joy Susan has never outgrown is searching for seashell treasures on every beach she visits! Soaking up sunny days, reading inspirational true stories and vacationing with family are also delightful to her soul.

Married for over 40 years, she loves quiet evenings and dinners with her husband.

www.ingramcontent.com/pod-product-compliance
Lightning Source LLC
Chambersburg PA
CBHW032227080426
42735CB00008B/748